C000067487

# In Praise of *God... It's Deedy. Can You Hear Me?*

Deedy has shared with the reader a story of innocence and innocence lost, of despair and hope, of trauma and healing, and of agonizing doubt and renewed faith. With amazing courage and grace, Deedy invites us into some of the darkest places of the human soul. While at the same time she sheds light on the tremendous resilience of the human spirit. There is also wonderful hope for each of us within these pages in knowing that even in the times of our lives we are most doubtful of God's presence, God is with us with each step of our journey,

This story represents the actual events as remembered by the author. Her recollections of how well-intentioned mental health practitioners of the past contributed to her re-traumatization do represent that which did, at times, occur prior to the advances of today,

Those readers who have experiences similar to Deedy's should take comfort in the knowledge that today there are very well developed, evidenced-based therapies for individuals who have been traumatized, These trauma-informed approaches recognize the need to provide safety, support, trustworthy collaboration, and empowerment for individuals healing from trauma. In addition, the newer medications available today assist in facilitating the treatment of trauma without the heavy tranquilizing and addictive consequences of the older medications described in this book.

Through Deedy's courage in telling her story of healing, may others rediscover their courage, hope, and faith as well.

Stephen M. Delisi, MD

ElderBerry Publishing
CMP Publishing Group, LLC

# God... It's Deedy

# Can You Hear Me?

By Deedy- Harmala

Copyright 2017 © Dorothy Harmala  All rights reserved.
No part of this book may be reproduced in any form, by photostat, microfilm, xerography, or any other means, or incorporated into any information retrieval system, electronic or mechanical, without the written permission of the author.

Cover Art by Deedy's Father, Winston Cordes

ElderBerry Publishing is a division of CMP Publishing Group, LLC. The focus of this division is on Community and family history.

All inquiries, including distributor information, should be addressed to:
Dorothy Harmala
email: deeharmala@gmail.com
  or
ElderBerry Publishing
27657 Highway 97
Okanogan, WA 98840
email: info@cmppg.org


ISBN13: 978-1-937162-14-6

Library of Congress Control Number: 2017955802

# Dedication

Now that my story is complete, I praise the Lord and thank Him for saving me and guiding me through the traumatic waves that flooded so much of my life.

Deep and lasting gratitude goes to my family and friends for their constant non-judgmental support and love through the various trials I faced as I grew into adulthood.

A very special thanks goes to my wonderful husband for convincing me to put my story down on paper and for standing by my side as I gained insight into my emotions and took control of my life. I believe Wayne is a gift from God and I love him deeply.

# Table of Contents

# Introduction

For more than 40 years, I have struggled to complete a very personal story. I finally feel ready to talk about my life's journey. As many people feel about their lives, I have survived tragedy, happiness, fear, pain, confusion, contentment, and love. The love of family, friends, workmates and an exceptional husband who stood with me through my struggles. I finally feel I have reached a place after a long and often disturbing journey where I see a glimpse of purpose, but even after living a long lifetime of years, it is only a glimpse! Like so many others, I have struggled with questions about my purpose, why am I here? Why did awful things happen to me? Are there things I need to do? Will I leave my world a better place because I existed? My search has been unending, a constant struggle to understand if my life has meaning other than to satisfy selfish desires.

My story began in 1948 when I was in a life changing accident at seven years of age. Before my accident, I was a little girl who grew up living near the beach in a small town called Santa Monica. My father was an architect and busy working at a firm in downtown Los Angeles, but when he got home, I was his little Princess. He doted on me and I loved the affection he gave me. My brother Ted always said I was our father's favorite child. I loved my father's attention and embraced the love he showered on me. My mother was a homemaker and took care of my brother Ted and me. She enjoyed preparing successful birthday parties for us and always invited as many kids as we wanted. These parties were so much fun that a very large crowd of children always attended. Mother also loved to entertain adults and would arrange elaborate galas at our home with many politicians and other influential people, along with family friends.

During the winter months my grandmother, whom I called Bambi, lived with us. She had been a very successful surgical doctor before her retirement. After retirement, she took up painting oil pictures of the ocean and beach, which she could view from her home in Laguna Beach. They were beautiful paintings with fine detailing and when looking at them, I could envision the warm sand beneath my feet and the sun beating down on me as I watched the large ocean waves crashing on the beach. When the weather on the coast became too cold for her to paint, she would come and stay with us, which was always a treat for my brother and me. We both adored her and spent many hours in her bedroom while she told us stories and sang to us. I loved sitting on her lap.

I had several close girlfriends living on my block with whom I played dolls and house. We prepared tea parties, played hide and seek, and ran through the sprinklers during the hot summer months. I was shy but never lonely and rarely alone. My life was very peaceful and full of fun activities with my family and friends. I felt loved, secure and cared for.

A few weeks after my thirteenth birthday, I was pulled into an event that cast me into a dark shadow that stayed with me for many years, causing anger and confusion. I had no counseling and shared my thoughts with no one. I felt that the Lord had ignored me and was angry with Him. The damage this caused to my self-image and self-worth culminated into a mental and emotional breakdown.

Even after I was in my thirties and the mother of three young boys I still struggled to find myself and held a silent anger at what I had gone through. Wayne, my husband of five years watched me shake and stammer when I tried to describe my experience. He understood that I needed to find answers and suggested I write my story down as a catharsis, which is how this story began to take form as a book.

Until a few months ago, I was unable to make myself complete my story and bring it to life on paper. One Sunday morning I was sitting in church and felt an overwhelming emotional need to ask God to give me a sign. Should I force myself through the painful emotions to complete the book or just put it aside? Perhaps it had served its purpose as a catharsis bringing me closure. With emotional tears filling my eyes, I prayed for a sign giving me an answer.

The next day, I received a phone call regarding a book publisher who might be interested in working with me to publish my book. Wow, was that a sign from God?

Many people knew about my story, and word of it reached Edna Siniff of ElderBerry Books. We met and talked and with Edna's guidance, my book is now a reality. Every day I prayed for God's help with my words. I am an avid reader, but not a writer and I needed all the help I could get.

The events in this book are what only I remember. I make no claim to the accuracy of the actual events, but the words are written as seen through my eyes and in my mind without input from others.

*Deedy at 9 years old. Her brother is in the background*

*Deedy, 7 years old, standing in front of the family home at the end of summer, before school began.*

*Deedy 10 years old and her brother Ted.*

# Chapter One

# Beginning of My Story

My story begins when I was seven years old and attending the second grade at Roosevelt grammar school. During the second week of school, the bell rang for recess and everyone sprung from their seats and headed out the door to the playground.

I was swinging from monkey bars with my friends when I fell onto my head in the sand below. The fall had stunned me and I lay in the warm sand for several minutes not sure if I was okay. With effort, I stood up and looking around became aware that the playground was empty and all my friends had returned to their rooms. I was unable to force my arm down from a bent position with my hand resting on the back of my neck but felt no pain. I slowly walked to the nurse's office where she told me to go back to my classroom and that I would be fine. When I came into the classroom and sat down, my teacher was concerned with the color or looks of my face and called my mother.

Luckily for me, I had a very loving and attentive mother who immediately called our family doctor. Doctor Dostal told my Mother that he suspected that I might have broken my neck. He cautioned her not to let me move. She called the school informing them to keep me sitting down and as still as possible, that I may have broken my neck and she and the doctor would be arriving at the school as soon as possible.

Within an hour, Mother and the doctor arrived. After my neck was examined it was determined that I had broken my neck and an ambulance was called to drive me to Santa Monica Hospital. After X-rays confirmed the diagnosis and due to the life threatening danger that often happened when a broken neck was set, a prominent orthopedic physician was called. He was well known because of his background of successfully setting bones during World War 11. I was kept immobile while he flew in from another state and went to work on my neck.

As a result of my accident, I was encased in a body cast which started directly below the lips of my mouth, covered my neck and shoulders and surrounded the core of my body continuing down to my hips, looking much like a sleeveless turtleneck shirt. I was also put into a wheelchair because I was unable to stand or use my legs. Because I walked into the nurse's office and back to my schoolroom, the doctors believed the use of my legs would return after they had time to rest and my neck healed.

This confinement lasted for a good portion of my next year into the following summer. My youthful age of seven prevented me from realizing how close death had come to take me away. I was unaware of how blessed I was in having a mother who possessed the patience of a saint. Since it was too difficult to take handicapped individuals into public places, I spent my entire healing time at home with a mother who took on the responsibility of becoming my teacher, my constant companion, and best friend. She guided me through the class work I was missing, keeping me busy with arts and crafts and reading. At this time in history, our world had no electronic devices to amuse ourselves with, and television did not exist in our homes. We entertained ourselves with board and card games. Our family also gathered around our grand piano as Mother or my brother Ted played songs to which we sang. As a family, we also spent many hours sitting around the table in our game room in conversation. We discussed everything from history to art to current news items and took turns telling jokes. In retrospect, my seventh year of life flew by as a spec in time.

Prior to my broken neck, I spent much of my early life in casts surrounding different parts of my body. My mother said I was 'accident-prone,' which I later learned was in part due to an abnormal inner ear that was the cause of my extremely poor balance. It wasn't until I was in my fifties that a medical examination disclosed that my lack of balance had a physical basis. I was not 'accident-prone,' my inner ears were malformed which made me physically unbalanced. I stopped trying to challenge myself in physical activities. I no longer had to try to prove I was not 'accident-prone' or careless or uncoordinated. This knowledge gave me a new way of viewing myself in relation to the world in which I moved. I learned to compensate for my lack of balance by using sight. I learned to focus on where my body was in relationship to the space around me, including the ground on which my feet stood. After over fifty years of falling, bumping, slipping, and contacting hard objects, I finally was able to navigate my way through the labyrinth of physical objects that are everywhere without colliding into them.

# Chapter Two

## Thirteen Years Old

The next trauma consumed my life from the age of thirteen until my very late teens. This event traumatically engulfed me as I was entering into my teenage years and tore away my childhood, filling me with loneliness and instability for many years to come. I felt I was alone with only confusion and anger at God for not stopping what happened next and came very close to becoming an atheist. I did, however, continue to pray. To this day, I carry the physical and emotional scars from this horrific event. For many years I lived with damage not only to my self-image and self-esteem but also to my permanent memory. All memory of life prior to this trauma disappeared or became very fuzzy, leaving me with almost no recollections of my childhood. Only stories from others and pictures in family scrapbooks have made it possible for me to see my childhood.

The memories I am writing down on paper of this event, are what only I remember and may not be the same as others remember. I make no claim to the accuracy of the actual events, but the words are written as seen through only my eyes and mind without input from others.

This memory won't go away and starts with me digging deeply into the skin of a man again and again. Even after the many years I have lived since that day, I can still feel the thickness of his skin pressing under my nails. I can still feel his hair as I grabbed it and pulled with all my strength. His hair was so slippery, so oily that my hands just slid away. I pushed his body and kicked hard, but the more I fought, the less I could move. He was big and his arms were everywhere. I could not free myself. His face was oily and dark. His mustache was greasy and dirty. Those dark, ugly eyes were so fierce that they pierced through me. His face was so close that I could smell it, a sickening, choking smell. As I held tightly to my coat I saw it getting torn to pieces. I tried to protect it, but could see it was being ruined forever. Terror consumed me.

When I opened my eyes, everything was black. I could feel the rough, damp ground against my face and pine needles were scratching my skin.

The dirt was hard, dark and cold and had a pungent odor. I couldn't get up or turn over. Other than the skin on my face, my body had no feeling. I tried to open my mouth, but it hurt. My throat felt as if I had been yelling loud and hard. My eyes felt swollen and sore. I must have been laying there for a long time when I heard someone say, "I'm going to make you ugly."

"Oh God NO" filled my thoughts with terror. I remembered the car and being pulled inside, fear filled me with a paralyzing force. My heart leaped to my throat, throbbing violently.

When I tried to breathe, I could not get enough air and was sure I would suffocate. Everything swirled in front of my eyes. When I tried to focus only hazy grays and whites swam before me. I was completely helpless and so very cold. I could not hear anything except that awful voice repeat over and over, "I'm going to make you ugly -- I'M GOING TO MAKE YOU UGLY!" Please God, I want to move, make him go away, help me, please someone help me, my thoughts cried out. My stomach hurt. My thoughts begged to be back home. The skin on my stomach felt torn and cold. I wanted Mother so much. My breasts felt pushed inside me. Each muscle in my body ached as though stretched to the breaking point. My arms were pulled from by body and tied to something close to the ground. My legs were tightly stretched wide apart from each other with my ankles tied to something. I tried to raise my head, but because I was tied so tight and securely I couldn't even look up. "I'M GOING TO MAKE YOU UGLY!" I was sure he was cutting me, but it did not hurt. Fear consumed me and whatever he was doing didn't feel painful. It must have been a long time when I opened my eyes again because everything was so dark and still. My body was shaking with uncontrollable violence. There was no pain, only a bitter coldness and overwhelming shaking.

A deeply felt quiet cry came out of my mind reaching to God for help; "Help me God, please help me." Then quiet nothingness and dark blackness again.

My eyes opened slowly. He wasn't there. I wasn't tied up. No one was there with me. I was alone in the dark with my face laying against the cold pine needle covered dirt. I failed when I tried to push myself up. My arms were too weak and stiff to support me. I rolled over on my back and looked up into the blackness. I saw the moon was full, and the sky was crowded with vivid stars. It was not nearly as dark as I thought. Thick trees closed over me making me feel that I was smothered deep down under darkness. The pine needles under my back felt like millions of tiny pins piercing my skin. I was cold - so icy cold. I turned my head to see my coat lying on the ground within reach, and I pulled it toward me. It too was cold, and as I covered myself with it the fabric felt wet and crusty. I could barely see through the blurring tears that were filling my eyes. I squeezed my lids shut as hard as I could and forced the tears away, again asking God for help. With a determined effort, I pushed myself up and put my arms into my coat, only to find one sleeve was nearly torn off. I looked down at what had been my new coat and again the tears filled my eyes. I loved my new coat and now it was ruined, forever ruined. I again squeezed the tears away and this time, I pleaded with God for help. I felt nothing and heard nothing and was sure God had not heard me. I was alone and terrified.

I knew I needed help, but was afraid to be seen by anyone. As tears continued to flow from my eyes, I looked around for my shoes, but could not find them. The coldness made it difficult for me to move, and a burst of uncontrollable spasms flew throughout my entire body. I was numb with no feelings, no awareness of any pain, only that awful persistent coldness and shaking. As I crawled my way out of the darkly crowded woods, I could see streetlights that illuminated a familiar looking area.

I ran to one of the homes that lined the street and thought I might be somewhere in the Santa Monica Mountains, maybe Mandeville Canyon or somewhere by Mulholland Drive. As I moved from house to house the area looked familiar, but I didn't recognize any of the rustic homes along the well-maintained neighborhoods. I heard a car and quickly ran for shelter behind a dark house, hiding myself. I was afraid to let anyone see me, yet knew I must find help. That constant cold shaking made it almost impossible for me to move as I looked up to God again asking for help. Panic forced me to push my legs into running from one hiding spot to another, as I held my coat tightly around me. It seemed like an eternity as I hid, then ran, then hid. I was so cold and tired I began to stumble and fell into a soft green carpet of grass. I pushed myself up and ran and hid, ran and hid again and again for what seemed like forever.

I was so cold and desperately wanted someone to help me when suddenly a familiar house appeared across the street. I ran to the front door and pounded on it with all my strength. It opened, and my friend Karen was standing there looking at me. She didn't move and as I saw her mouth open, she became fuzzy and small to my eyes. Then I saw the ground rush toward me through a swirling haze, and I grasped onto my coat for protection.

14

Chapter Three

# What Really Happened?

Upon waking up I felt a rush of hot fear sweeping through my head and lodge in my throat. A wet coldness ran down my arms and legs and left me shaking as though I had a vibrating machine inside me. I pushed my legs down stiffly against the bed I was laying on to try to stop the shaking. The world was swirling around me. I shut my eyes pressing the lids tightly together to stop the world from going around and around. I kept my eyelids shut tightly together for a while longer until the shaking seemed to be under control. When I opened them again, Mother was standing next to my bed smiling down at me. Seeing her flooded me with confusion as my eyes filled up and tears began pouring down my face. Her strong arms encircled me with a gentle firmness, and somehow I felt safer. My body shook as I cried until I was empty. While she held me with her warm love, I tried to push the confusing memories of that awful man away from my mind. His awful smell was still in my nose and I could still feel his eyes piercing through me.

"Oh, my darling girl, you're alright now. It's all over. We were so worried. Now you're back with us and you are going to be fine."

I tried to talk, but my voice just made me choke. The shivering coldness I felt was back inside me. My shaking would not stop. Mother seemed to know how cold I was without me saying anything, and she covered me with more blankets and held me tightly again. Gradually, I began to feel safe, as the shaking slowly left my legs. After it was gone, I felt weak and empty. I looked around the room that surrounded me, and everything was clean and white, so very different from him. I could not see anyone who would hurt me now.

A nurse came in and gave me a shot that quickly filled me with flowing warmth. The warm feeling was wonderful and soon I floated away on the bed.

When I again opened my eyes and looked around I was overwhelmed by the whiteness of the room surrounding me. The walls, floor, ceiling and sheets seemed so clean and simple. Bouquets of bright flowers were on the table and gave the room an impression of happiness. Everything was so quiet, peaceful, and clean. I finally felt safe and hoped I could forget that awful man. He was gone. I would not think about him again. He was gone forever!

"Where's Daddy?"

"He'll be back later, dear."

When I heard Mother's voice answer me, it seemed to be far away and sounded as though it was not in the room, but far from everything around me. As I floated away, I was sure I was dreaming. It was a good warm feeling.

When I woke up, Mother was still there and asked if I felt better. I did. As she got up from the edge of my bed, I wondered how long she had been there.

She walked over to the nearest bouquet of flowers, taking the card from it, she said,

"Your friends have sent you some beautiful flowers, Deedy."

As I looked at them, I wondered where my brother was and asked if he'd been to visit me. Mother told me Ted didn't like hospitals and didn't want to see me in one. She went on saying that hospitals made him feel sick, and he'd rather wait till I came home. A heavy feeling of disappointment came over me. I was sure Ted was the smartest person in the world because he was three and a half years older than me and he read all the time. He was a senior at Santa Monica High School and got all A's on his report cards. I wanted to hear him say everything was all right. I turned my face away from Mother not wanting her to see me cry again.

After a few minutes, Mother's voice broke the peaceful silence, sending the room spinning in front of my eyes. Then I heard her say, "The investigating police officer will be in to see you this afternoon, Deedy." I felt as though I was falling through the bed; I couldn't talk about what had happened. When I thought about his horrible eyes and choking smell, my throat filled up with a nauseating thickness that made it hard for me to breathe. I crawled under the covers and pushed my head against the pillow. I didn't want to hear her words.

Again, Mother seemed to know my thoughts without my having said anything, and she wrapped her arms around me and said, "You have to tell the police everything you can about what happened. I know you probably don't want to talk about it Deedy, but you must help them so they can apprehend him. We can't allow that kind of person to be free to hurt someone else."

My body started to shiver again while in my brain knew she was right. The problem was I couldn't talk about how awful he was, his oiliness, his smell, and his voice. I did not want to think about it or talk about it ever again. It was over and I was going to erase the memory forever. As I felt warm sweat start on the back of my neck and trickle down my back, I remembered how cold I had been.

"The police will be nice Deedy, don't worry. They understand what you've been through. They just have to find out what he looked like if they are going to find him."

# Chapter Four

# I Won't Think About It!

I pressed my head against the pillow and wrapped it around to the side of my face trying to cover my other ear. I would not think about it. I would only think about my friends in Lincoln Junior High School. Our group of girls had so much fun together. We had a club consisting of about 25 girls and used the poodle as our symbol. Just last Easter we had an Easter Hat contest. My friend Suzy and I each made an actual Easter basket full of colorful eggs and flowers. We balanced our baskets on our heads with satin ribbons tied in big bows under our chins. Everyone loved our design and we won first prize. The memory brought a smile to my lips.

My smile faded as I remembered that someone from the police department would be coming this afternoon and would want me to talk about that awful man.

Until the investigator arrived that afternoon, I lay in bed with a deep dread of what was to come. I tried to think of other things. Of happy, worry-free times with my friends, but my mind kept returning to when he would walk in. I have no idea what I expected him to be like, but when he walked in his appearance surprised me. He looked like a businessman in his gray suit and white shirt, which was something like Daddy might wear to work. When I first saw him that dreadful feeling of apprehension left until he started the questions. They came so fast. I hardly had a chance to answer one before he interrupted me with another.

I attempted to tell him about walking to the mailbox after school to mail a letter, but he cut me short and said, "Then what?" I told him I had been crossing the street to where the box was when a car came around the corner and I stopped to wait for it to pass by me. Everything seemed so vivid to me as I was talking, almost as though it was happening again, right now.

"I remember the door of the car suddenly opened and someone grabbed me. That's all I remember of the car."

Then I heard the investigator say, "Did you scream?" Before I could

18

answer, he asked if I fought the man at that time.

"I don't remember. I know I fought him as hard as possible, but I can't remember anything more about the car. The next thing I remember was being in the woods." My legs began to shake again, and I could feel that same coldness I had felt in the woods. My voice sounded to me as though it was coming from someone else, except that it echoed in my head.

I tried to tell the investigator about being tied down. And about not being able to move.

He interrupted me again and asked where the man had taken me. I told him "I don't know. He had me tied down on the ground so tightly I couldn't even raise my head. My legs and arms were tied to something and that awful man kept saying "I'm going to make you ugly over and over again. I was so very cold the whole time. Pine needles were poking in my face and the dirt was cold and wet against my skin. I was sure he was doing something to my body, but I didn't feel any pain. I don't know what he did to me. I only know he was horrible and wanted to hurt me."

Then the investigator said the strangest thing, which I could not understand. He asked me if I had met that awful man before, and did he know where I lived. The investigator's voice became fuzzy and distant to my ears. Everything was confusing. There were too many blank spaces in my memory, too many things I couldn't remember. How could he ask me if I had ever met that awful man before? What kind of a question was that? He was an awful man. Why did he make me feel I had done something wrong? That maybe I did something wrong or should have fought harder or screamed louder? I could hear him asking if I screamed. His voice began to fade away and his face became blurry and unreal, like a mask. How could he think I knew anyone as terrible as that awful man?

"I don't know anyone like him! He was horrible and I don't know people like that!" I whispered. Tears spilled out of my eyes and I couldn't look at the investigator anymore.

Then he asked me, "When did you fight and do you remember screaming?"

"Why do you ask those questions? I don't remember." I stammered through my tears. Then I heard my voice crying out loudly, saying words so fast they tumbled over each other.

"He was so greasy so dirty I fought him as hard as I could. He had awful eyes that looked through me. I kicked him but it just didn't do

19

any good. The more I fought him the less I could move. I screamed and screamed, but no one heard me. He had me tied so tightly to the ground that I couldn't even lift my head. He just wanted to make me ugly or something. I don't know why he took me away. I was so cold, so awfully cold. I just wanted to be back home. It was awful oh it was awful AWFUL!! Please, I can't talk about it anymore - don't make me talk about it - please, please don't ask any more questions. I can't talk about it anymore."

After my voice stopped, I felt drained. The investigator said, "We know you must be a pretty good little fighter, and I'll bet you left some great scratches on him." He continued telling me that when they found me, there was skin and hair under my nails that they were keeping for evidence. Then he asked if I had also fought during intercourse.

His face went fuzzy and I was sure I didn't hear him right. I know I didn't. He was confused and not making any sense. I was barely able to get my question out, "What are you talking about? What do you mean?"

They knew I had intercourse, he said, from the evidence the doctor found. I was dizzy and clammy all over and that icy cold shaking returned, making my muscles jerk and jump. My head was hot, but my body was so very cold.

"How can you talk like that?" I blurted out, "It's not true and you don't know what you're talking about." He was wrong! I was sure. I would remember THAT, even if I didn't remember everything - I'd remember THAT! "All that happened was I was tied down and he tried to make me ugly and I fought him. That's all that happened," I stammered in a whispering voice.

"You don't remember having intercourse?" He asked.

"NO -NO -NO, that did not happen!"

"When it happens to a girl against her will, it is called rape. Is that how it happened?"

His persistent questions smothered me.

"NO NO that never happened." I was shaking so hard now that I could not talk anymore, so I turned my back to him and pressed my face into my pillow.

After the investigator got up and left the room, I curled up on my side and held the pillow close to my body the way I used to hold my doll. The more I shook, the closer I held my doll. Tears were running down the side of my nose and into my mouth. They tasted good and salty. I could feel the pillow getting wet. Then a nurse came in and gave me another shot. Soon I was floating again and as I held on tightly to my doll I felt better.

I don't know how long I had been floating when Mother came in. I was glad to see her. Now she would tell me that the investigator was confused and wrong. After describing what he had said, I waited for a long time before she said anything. As she responded, her voice sounded far away. She said the doctor had examined me when they brought me to the hospital and found evidence of intercourse.

My voice was yelling inside my head - NO NO NO.

She held me close in her arms saying, "It doesn't matter, darling."

I pushed her away. Not Mother too - she couldn't believe the investigator was right, not Mother. I knew things like that did happen to other girls. Not me. If it had happened to me, I would know. I would remember that! How could I not know if it had happened? They have to be wrong.

# Chapter Five

# No! No! That Didn't Happen!!

My voice was barely audible as I said, "Mother, the investigator made me feel bad like I did something wrong. I don't want to see him again. He even asked me if I knew the man and if the man knew where I live. His questions didn't make any sense and he made me feel as though I did something wrong like maybe I didn't fight hard enough. Mother, I was not raped. I'd remember that. I know I would. I can't talk to him again."

She put her hands on the sides of my face and turned it toward hers, all the time looking into my eyes and said, "It doesn't matter darling, you must believe me. Don't let anything he said upset you." She stopped long enough to brush the tears from her cheek and continued, "There is no way any of this is your fault. You were just unlucky to be there when he drove by. Deedy, you were just at the wrong place at the wrong time." She was crying now as she put her arms around me and held so tight it almost hurt. She took my face in her hands again and looking into my eyes said, "You're alright now darling, you're safe and it's all over. We must put the entire event behind us and move forward toward a future full of good things. Whatever happened is unimportant in the big picture of life. You must believe me that the only important thing that has happened is that you are alive and you are going to be fine."

Her face looked old and tired; her eyes were red and puffy and her cheeks were wet. She hugged me for a long time until gradually I felt calmer even though the fear lingered that Mother would never believe me. The investigator had somehow convinced her that I had been raped.

As she held me, I closed my eyes and saw myself a couple of years ago playing in the backyard with Cheri. We were playing hide and seek and running in and out behind the playhouse in my backyard. It was a beautiful playhouse the size of a regular room and all the kids loved to play in my yard because of it. On each side of the front door, it had pale blue shuttered windows. The front porch was large enough for two chairs and a table on which we served tea. Cheri was my best friend and was the only girl on my block who would play dolls. Most of my friends didn't play dolls anymore since they became interested in boys. I could see myself laughing and having such a good time with Cheri. We didn't have anything to worry about then. I floated along in my memories for the longest time, until I fell asleep.

*Deedy holding one of the dolls she and Cheri played with.*
*Few memories from Deedy's childhood survived.*
*One is this dress. A red and white checked pinafore.*

Later, that evening Daddy came to see me. To my bewilderment, when he came into my room and I looked at his face he looked much older than I remembered. His expression was full of sadness and he looked like I could imagine he might if I had died. He seemed sad and far away from me. When he took my hand in his and kissed my forehead he seemed very formal. As he looked at me he seemed so far away, like I was not 'his favorite daughter' now even though he held my hand. I don't think he wanted to be there. As I watched him, I felt his behavior toward me was different than it used to be. I didn't feel any warmth from him and it made me feel terribly uncomfortable. I felt he was examining me when he looked at me or that he was looking for something to be different. I became aware of an undefined guilt and shame inside me. That clamminess down the middle of my back returned again and I wished he would leave.

He asked, "How's my princess?"

"I'm fine Daddy,"

"Do those bruises on your face hurt?" He asked as he looked my direction.

"Where? I didn't know I had any bruises."

I asked him to hand me a mirror and as I peered into it, my legs began to shake against the mattress. I had trouble holding the mirror still as I examined two brown eyes circled with ugly blue and red puffy skin. The face looking out at me was sort of like mine. The mouth was mine except it looked scrapped as though it was rubbed with gravel or sandpaper. The long blond hair was dirty and tangled with dark stuff stuck in it and matted down. My eyes burned. An awful thickness filled my throat again and made me choke. It took a huge effort to get my words out,

"Will it go away? I want to look like I used to?"

"Yes darling," Mother said, "those are just surface bruises and they'll be gone in a few weeks. You'll look just fine in a short time. The cuts on your body will take a while longer to heal, especially the ones on your back. The doctor thinks he used a razor blade."

I hadn't felt the cuts on my body or back before, but now after hearing Mother tell me about them it felt as if they were piercing my skin, and I was stiff and sore all over. A tightness filled my stomach like a knot. Then I remembered my beautiful new black coat that I had been wearing when I went to mail that letter. I asked Mother where it was, and she told me the police were keeping it for evidence. Every inch of me felt empty, abandoned of all feeling. I knew I'd never see my coat again and that it was ruined and would not be returned. Nothing was the same as it had been before that awful man came. He ruined my coat and he ruined me. Everything was ruined and out of order and all mixed up. Gravity was pulling my body down. All my strength had left and I didn't attempt to talk. I turned my back to Mother and Daddy and buried myself under the safety of my covers.

As my parents got ready to leave, a nurse came in and gave me some little yellow pills that made me float again. I was learning to enjoy that floating feeling. My body was warm and somehow nothing mattered when I was floating. I wasn't even aware that Mother and Daddy had left.

Waking up the next morning, I was sure that the things in my memory did not happen. They were only from a bad dream. I would lock them away in my brain where no one could reach them. They will be locked safely away forever.

I realized Mother was sitting in the chair next to my bed and wondered if she had been there all night. I was glad she was my Mother, always sure of herself and very smart. I admired her so much and was sure she was the most brilliant woman ever. She was involved in politics, which I thought was a man's world. She told me that women could handle political situations as well, if not better than men could. She was probably right; she usually was. Mother did not have to leave the house to work as so many of my friend's mothers did. After school, I brought friends home for snacks, which Mother always had ready, no matter how many friends came home with me. All my friends loved my Mother and said I was so lucky to have a Mom who stayed home with me. Some days Connie and I baked cookies and made a big mess, but Mother never criticized us. I loved my Mother so much and thought about how lucky I was. Connie's mother was so different that I felt sorry for her. Her mother only thought about her looks and her boyfriends. Connie had to baby sit for her younger sisters while her mother went out on dates at night. She seemed to me to be so selfish.

My Mother was nothing like that but instead seemed to thrive on taking care of me, my brother, my Dad and Bambi. All those weekends after Connie moved out to the valley during the seventh grade, Mother and I would drive out to get her on Friday afternoon. She would stay with us until we drove her home on Sunday night. The only complaint I had about Mother was that she was overweight and didn't spend enough time on her looks. I remembered seeing pictures of her when she was in her twenties and she was beautiful. I wondered why so many mothers became overweight when they got older.

As I watched Mother sitting in the chair a warm feeling of love filled me reminding me of how much care and concern she and Daddy always showed toward us. We were lucky to have such parents. Many of my friends came from divorced parents who were too busy to spend time with them. Daddy has said I am a lot like Mother. He called her princess too. Daddy still called me a little girl, even though I would be fourteen on my next birthday.

My stomach was growling from lack of food, so I told Mother I was hungry. She looked up from her book and said,

"Well that sounds good. Let's get some food for you."

As she went out to find a nurse, I thought about Connie and our warm friendship. When Mother came back in I asked if Connie had called.

"No, honey, she hasn't." Her answer gave me a heavy feeling of disappointment. Then the nurse came in bringing a tray full of a soft-boiled egg with crackers and a paper cup of vanilla ice cream. I ate every bite as my thoughts of Connie drifted away.

Between each spoonful, I asked Mother "How long have I been here? More than one day?"

"This is your third day in the hospital, Deedy."

"Really? When did it happen? When did I mail that letter?"

She replied, "You went to the mailbox Friday evening, which was four days ago and finally showed up at Karen's house late Saturday night."

I asked her "What day is today?"

"Today is Tuesday."

"Oh dear, what about school? I'm missing school. I'll have lots of work to make up. How long will I be here?"

"You'll probably be here a couple more days. Then we'll see how you feel. Don't worry about school. This morning I talked to your teachers and they understand what happened. They want to help any way they can. They don't want you to worry."

The thought of my teachers knowing what happened to me brought a hot feeling to my face, as though I had a fever.

What if they have heard about what the investigator said? How could I ever go back to school and face them again? I wished as hard as I could that no one else had heard, not my teachers, not my friends - no one. I thought about graduating from the eighth grade next June and was glad that my teachers were willing to help me. I didn't want anything to prevent my becoming a senior in Junior High next year with all my friends.

An image of one of the boys I really liked named Brian came to my mind, and I asked Mother if he had called.

"Yes, he called you twice today and wanted to know when he could visit you. How would you feel about your friends coming tomorrow afternoon?"

"Well, I want to see them, but don't you think it would be better if they didn't see me with my face so messed up? Maybe they should wait for a few days?"

Shortly after lunch, another policeman came in to talk to me. When he told me he had some questions for me to answer, I decided nothing he might say could bother me; that I would be strong and objective, as if we were talking about some story I read. This man turned out to be much different from the investigator and didn't make me feel bad. His questions were easy and he had a gentle manner about him.

He showed compassion when he said, "I understand you had a rough time."

"Yes." I agreed and waited for his next sentence.

"What do you remember? Tell me as much as you can."

I was determined to remain strong and objective, but that clamminess under my arms and down my back was making me nervous. As I talked, my voice sounded unreal to me, as though it belonged to someone else, but the words were mine. I dragged through every memory filling my mind, including the horrible coldness. I was aware that I had an intense fear of that coldness and each time I had to talk about it, the coldness came back stronger than before. It was almost as though it was happening again. I went on to describe the man. I told him the man had said, "I'm going to make you UGLY" when he was trying to hurt me.

But the policeman intervened with a kind compliment, "You're a very pretty girl, and I'm glad he didn't succeed."

After hearing my account of what happened, he informed me that the police were scouting the area around Karen's house to find any evidence that might still be there. They were trying to locate the spot where that man had taken me.

The investigator would be back later, he said, to talk to me some more. Another bolt of iciness shot through me at these words. I was so sure I could lock what had happened away and hide it in my brain, but it didn't work.

After he left, I crawled deep under my blankets looking for a little bit of warmth to stop the shaking.

Mother came in and I asked her if I had to talk to that awful investigator again.

"Haven't I told them everything? Why would they come back? I really don't want to keep going over it."

She said sympathetically, "Don't let anything either of them has said bother you. They are just doing their jobs, even though they may not be very diplomatic about it."

I lay there thinking about any of them returning and knew I had to find some hidden strength. It would be necessary in order to survive all the painful intrusions into that awful memory that would be better off dead and buried. No one would let me forget it. Each time I thought it was over and buried, someone made me relive it again. Even though people had constantly been coming and going, in and out of my room, I felt so very much alone. I decided to steel myself against those intrusions from the investigators by pretending that it was not me who was taken away, but someone else. I would not talk about myself; instead there would be a third person who I could talk about, maybe someone from a book I had read, or from a bad dream I'd had.

This time, the confrontation with the investigator's questions was much easier. He brought several large books full of pictures of scary looking men for me to try to identify. Many of the men pictured looked something like he had, but none of them were exactly right.

The investigator asked, "If I come back later with a police artist who will draw a picture of the man from your description, can you describe him clearly and with detail?"

"I'll try. I remember his oily hair, his mustache, and his smell. I remember he had a big face and was very dirty. I'll do my best to describe him."

As he walked out the door, I felt relief and wished somehow he would not return again. But a couple of hours later just as before, my wish went unanswered and he returned. The chubby, balding man who came with him was nice enough and didn't ask me anything except about the man's looks.

"The eyes were so black, so dark, but with an eerie sort of shine in them, as though they were lighted from within. Dumb. He seemed dumb and he talked like a dumb person, as though he hadn't been to school or ever read anything. His mustache was greasy and dirty and smelled. All of him smelled. His hair felt so slippery with oil and was thick, wet and smelly. I tried to pull his hair as hard as I could but my hands just slid away. I'm pretty sure his skin was dark and thick. It's hard for me to describe it because what I remember is how useless it was to try to dig my nails into his face because the skin wouldn't give. It was tough and rubbery like a slippery inner tube. His face seemed huge and smelled awful, something like old tobacco and dirt. I think he must have been a really big person such as a muscle man and very greasy and dirty."

"No more." I begged. "I can't talk about him anymore."

"Please, Deedy, is there anything else? Did he limp? Or maybe you remember a scar or a tattoo. Did he have any marks you can remember?" The investigator just wouldn't let me alone.

"No." I answered.

The artist waited for a few minutes as if he expected me to say more and then held the picture up in front of me. It was a good drawing and looked quite a lot like him, except something was missing. It just wasn't him, maybe because the feel of his skin was missing or the slipperiness of that greasy hair or that awful smell or the sound of his voice. On paper it was only a face, maybe his face, maybe not. Without his awful voice and the fierce eyes peering through me the image in front of me was reduced to a drawing on paper. As the artist put away his pencils and paper I expected the investigator to get up and leave too, but instead he just sat there. When I realized he was going to stay, my head began to pulse hotly with a beat and my mouth felt dry. I could not talk, not one word or sound would come out of my mouth. My tongue was so thick and dry it felt like it was sticking to the roof of my mouth. There was nothing left to say. I was empty inside; completely drained of everything.

As I looked blankly through him, he asked, "Would you go over what happened again?"

Then I heard a third person saying, "I already told you the whole story."

"Please Deedy, maybe you'll remember something else. Do you have any memory of being raped? Has that come back to you yet?" He pursued.

I just kept looking through him and soon he got up and left. For a long time, I laid there digging deeply into my mind to recall every buried detail. A faint image emerged of Dr. Dostal putting something up in me between my legs, which hurt. When I had gone to the bathroom this morning and all day yesterday, it burned. The insides of my thighs felt raw and bruised when I walked. Oh God, please don't let it be true, no matter what anyone says, please - please?

As I begged in my thoughts, I saw a bride dressed in a beautiful white dress floating away from me. Please God, I want to have children. I want to get married. Mother came in and saw me huddled deep under my covers for warmth.

"Mother, please tell me it isn't true. I wasn't raped."

Her words were wrong and I trembled when I heard them.

"Deedy, you were raped. I realize you don't remember it and that is probably best. It doesn't matter what he might have done to you. You are alive and you will be fine. We thank God you are here with us now and it's time to move on to the future."

"You weren't there, how do you know?" I whispered.

"Dr. Dostal found evidence when he examined you. He said there did not appear to be any permanent damage. You will soon be fine and you will grow up, fall in love, get married and become a mother." Her answer entered my ears and filled my insides with the heaviness of lead, yet at the same time, my head was spinning with a lightness.

My voice echoed, "I'm not a virgin anymore?"

"Darling, don't worry about that. It's not important, you're alive, and you'll fully recover." She went on and on and on, "You have a good future ahead of you Deedy. Someday you will fall in love with a man who will understand what happened to you was not your fault, that you lost your virginity against your will and not voluntarily. You will still have all those children you have talked about and be happy. I know your Father and I taught you that a girl should remain a virgin until after she is married, but this is different. It was just a tragedy that you got caught up in and we are very thankful you're alive."

All the time she kept talking, she was hugging me and crying. She brushed her hands through my hair and kissed the side of my head.

I never tried to say anything because I knew she was wrong, but would never believe me. I shut off her voice and the feel of her arms. Just before she left, I told her I didn't want to wait any longer for my friends to visit and that I didn't care how my face looked. I wanted to see them tomorrow. That night I had a horrible dream about being a bad girl, just like Charlotte at school, who let all the boys do what they wanted with her. I dreamed that I got pregnant and had to stop going to school. I had a baby that was little but had a big head that looked just like that awful man. I dreamed that all my friends were on the other side of a fence and whispering and pointing at me. My baby had a razor in his hand and was saying "ugly mommy."

# Chapter Six

# Back To School

Three weeks had passed since it happened, and I was finally returning to school. Nightmares and fear had taken over my nights. What would I face when I saw all my friends? They had not visited me in the hospital after all. They told Mother they would wait until I was back home.

After being at home a couple of days, they finally did visit. They were very nice to me and didn't ask any embarrassing questions, which made me feel better about returning to school.

Mother picked up make-up assignments from my teachers and I tried to push myself through them. It was hard for me to concentrate and I had to fight my mind from wondering back to that horrible event. School no longer seemed important to me. I could not find reasons to care about learning history, social studies, or math or any other subjects I would face in school. These subjects no longer seemed important to me. It was too hard to focus when reading about things I couldn't care less about. I had changed and my life was different now. Everything had changed.

On the morning of my first day, as I was getting ready a mixture of anticipation and foreboding filled me. I dressed carefully choosing just the right clothes. I decided to wear my brown and beige skirt, which came four inches below my knees, and the soft pink sweater that fit so perfectly. After I tied a brown scarf around my neck, I looked down at my white bucks, which were bright with fresh powder. I was satisfied. I combed my hair until each strand was smooth and in its proper place and used hair spray to make sure everything would stay put. Upon closer examination of the faint traces left by the bruises and cuts on my face, I decided to add a touch of powder. Only a light bluish-yellow shadow remained under my eyes that I couldn't completely hide.

I went into Mother's room to look in her full-length mirror for a better view of myself, to make my final judgment. I stood there studying the reflection, unable to determine why my image appeared so different than I remembered. I pressed my face closer to the mirror, almost touching it with my nose and could see my breath fogging the glass. The face peering at me appeared strange and seemed to belong to someone else; it looked too old to be mine. My face had always had a soft, innocent clean-cut look about it; the face in the mirror was hard and much too serious. My figure would never fit with that face. It needed a curvy, adult figure, like Julie London's. I stepped back, turned sideways and held my stomach in as tight as I could. My breasts looked much bigger now, and when I stood with all my weight on one leg, thrusting my hip forward, the figure was transformed into one that could go with the face. Except the shoes, they were too white and flat. High heels; very high would be better. The unfamiliar image staring out at me was disturbing and projected an impression completely alien to the one I had always strived to project; one that was clean-cut and had that all-American look. Bucks were especially popular now, with their fresh whiteness. The stranger reflected in the mirror would be considered a bad girl and not acceptable to my group. I closed my eyes, rubbing the lids to wash away that image and when I opened them was relieved to see my old familiar self. With a grain of self-confidence restored, I turned slowly, checking again to make sure everything was where it should be.

As Mother drove me to school, I was filled with a discomforting mixture of excitement and fear. I secretly hoped that no one had heard the awful lies that came from the investigator. As I started to get out of the car, Mother reached over and patted my legs saying, "Relax honey and smile Deedy, you will be fine."

Feeling awkward and conspicuous, I made my way to the special area where the eighth-graders gathered. As hundreds of eyes watched me, and heads turned my direction, I put a big smile on my face and held my head up high imagining myself as a princess going down a red carpet. Or was I Hester going to town, from the book I read last semester called, 'Scarlet Letter'? Beads of perspiration on my lip and nose were distracting as I looked down at my breast. There was no scarlet letter, and I could find nothing out of place. Why was everyone staring; what were they looking at? The faces, so many faces were all fuzzy; except the eyes. Eyes, thousands of them, were clearly defined and glaring at me. They knew! They must know! Why else would they be staring at me? The whole school knew, and they believed it too! My face was burning hot, my heart was pounding in my ears, and I wished with all my might that I would vanish. I desperately wanted to run, but my body kept moving in the same direction. I walked and walked, still holding my head up and my stomach in through that torturous crowd when suddenly I heard

Susan's voice beside me. Then with great relief, I felt her arm encircle my shoulder.

Thank God, I don't have to be alone now. A feeling of love for Susan pushed through my turbulent emotions. She kept her protective arm around my shoulder, reassuringly and supportive, as we walked.

Sensing my desire for quiet, she didn't talk. Soon other kids began to swarm around us and then the questions began.

"How are you Deedy?" "We missed you, how do you feel?" "You look fine, are you O.K?"

Before I had to answer them, the first bell rang, and soon the crowd dissolved. Susan walked with me to my first class without asking a single question. Her only comment was that Brian had been looking for me.

The days slowly dragged on until the first Friday at the end of my first week arrived. Even though I had been back to school for only one week, the time had passed like an eternity. Too many prying questions, too many staring eyes. I had become an oddity. The kids in my group had been very curious and persistent with their questions. I had not been able to talk about what happened or answer any questions. It was nice to find out that they had remained faithful friends and continued to include me in all the activities, just as before. Except things were not the same for me, nothing was the same. I wished they would stop asking questions and staring. I didn't feel like I belonged with them anymore. I was too self-conscious and felt so agitated. They hadn't changed; they still did the same things they had done before it happened. No, I was the one who was different. They behaved as they always had, still the leaders and most popular students, the cheerleaders, football and baseball players, student council members, and on and on. Our group had always been looked upon by other students as 'The Group' to belong to and the one in which to make friends. We were friendly with everyone and would accept anyone into our group if they showed interest. We did have small sub-clusters within the large group, but in general each of us was nice to everyone. Many of us had been to school together since kindergarten and then there were always new students entering into school who became part of our group. It would be nice to feel comfortable within my group again, but I was too different from everyone else now. That awful man had changed everything and the investigator's lies had turned me into a curious object, someone to stare at.

Another week of never-ending discomfort passed as I sat in class hearing Mr. Blum's monotonous explanation concerning some problem.

I hated the constant feeling of being a spectacle and knew that the kids talked behind my back. I was also quite positive that not only had everyone in the whole school heard I was raped, but that they believed it too. Day after day came and went, and I wished that I didn't have to sit in this or any other class. Every day and every class ran into the next one until they all blended into a confusing mess. I didn't care about math, history, English, civics or any of that other gibberish my teachers spewed out. I only wished to be in my nice, safe room at home and away from the staring eyes.

I jumped when I felt a hand tapping my shoulder from behind. "Hey, Deedy, Mr. Blum just asked you."

I turned my head slightly and asked, "What did he ask?"

The student behind me replied, "The answer to problem six."

I looked up at the teacher; everyone was looking at me again and waiting quietly for something.

"I don't know," I answered, giving my usual reply.

I felt that uncontrollable moisture trickling down my back; my hands were warm and clammy, and I was sure my blouse had big wet marks under the arms. I felt so conspicuous. Why couldn't it be like it was before it happened? Why had everything become so confusing and uncomfortable? If only that awful man and what he did to me could be erased forever. I wanted those scars to vanish and to be pretty again.

I heard the bell ring with relief. Now I could go, and maybe I would feel more comfortable in the next class. Maybe the kids wouldn't stare at me, and maybe the teachers wouldn't be so patronizing, as though doing me a favor. When I got up to leave, I held my arms down close to my sides so no one could see the wet marks I was sure were on my blouse.

After school, Susan grabbed me saying, "We're stopping at the 'Sweet Sixteen' restaurant for ice cream cones on the walk home." Susan and I walked home together most days since we had lived our whole lives on the same block on Tenth Street and were great friends. The 'Sweet Sixteen' restaurant was on 14th Street and down several blocks. We got there as the kids were laughing and planning a car wash for Saturday at Susan's house. I felt a pang of sadness as the image of past car washes flashed through my mind. They had been such fun with all the squirting of water getting us soaking wet. We usually ended up with all of us running around chasing each other with water buckets full of soap suds.

As I sat in a booth full of friends, I felt transparent as though no one could see me while I licked my ice cream cone. I watched what they were doing and heard them, but when they talked to me, it was as though they were talking through me to someone else. I couldn't find meaning in the world they talked about, and it didn't seem connected to mine. I couldn't relate to them and found it hard to remember I used to feel like part of this group. I was aware they didn't realize I was not the same person I was before that man took me away. Only in my room at home did I belong; away from their buzzing voices; free from pretending things were unchanged.

The laughter surrounding me jolted my awareness to the fact that I was laughing. I had no idea what the laughing was about when Jean said, "Boy, Deedy, you're sure right about that." It was just another time like so many recently when I had no idea of what was going on around me or of what I might have said. I was determined, unless Susan forced me to go, I would not join the car wash at her house next Saturday.

That afternoon, upon reaching the safety of my bedroom, I became transformed into an unconfused girl who was free from prying eyes. The cold, clammy sweatiness of my body that betrayed me at school disappeared. I lay on my bed staring at the ceiling, watching myself in a beautiful white dress float in a cloud with a handsome man holding my hand. We were getting married, and I would always be in love with him because he would spend his whole life loving all of me. The whiteness of the dress was a symbol of my purity and goodness.

As the days went by, somehow I managed to struggle through two more weeks, routinely going from class to class or making those miserable trips to the police station with Mother, but always in an emotionless trance with a smile on my face.

# Chapter Seven

## He Wasn't Real

When at the police station I watched men walk across the stage and felt as though I wasn't sitting there. I couldn't feel the chair under me, or the floor when I pushed my feet down hard against the insides of my shoes. I had no feeling in my body, only in my mind. The men in front of me were not nice looking, and if I thought about them, I would become disturbed and confused again. It was a good thing that I was able to sit in the dark where no one could see me. My chair was placed behind a large glass window that I looked through to see several men as they walked onto a stage and then stood still looking in my direction. What I was told was that they could not see me through the glass, that it looked like a mirror to them on their side. I've been here four times, and he has never been on the stage. I knew he never would be either because he had become unreal to me. I had made him disappear. When the investigator had those men talk, they all sounded alike. The investigator thought that I might recognize a voice, so he had them each say, "I'm going to make you ugly." His voice was never there. Sometimes those men looked alike, as though they were produced in a factory and not real. If I tried to concentrate on them, I would only become confused, so I didn't. The investigator said I was a cooperative girl. He had no idea of how miserable I felt looking at those faces and hearing those voices. I hated going to the police station and saw the way the policemen looked at me. The voices in the room and behind the glass became blurry and fuzzy, but I still kept a smile on my face so no one would know my feelings.

I knew what the policemen thought. Somehow, just because the investigator said I was raped, everyone believed it was true. If it had been true, and I had been raped by that awful man, he wouldn't have let me live. My mind told me a thousand times that only bad girls survived rape and that was because they cooperated. I knew I didn't cooperate with anything, and the investigator even said they had evidence that proved I fought hard. Good girls didn't live after what they said I went through, but I was alive, so I knew they were wrong. I could feel the chair under me now, and was aware of the musty air in the room. I pushed my toes against the insides of my shoes so hard that I got a cramp in the arch of my foot. It must be over since the men were leaving the stage. As I watched them walk under the bright lights that were directly over the stage, I felt dirty and full of shame. I wanted to disappear, not to have to face that investigator again. My body felt conspicuous; so much in the way, so ugly and out of control.

The investigator's voice broke the silence, "Well, Deedy did you recognize any of them?"

I felt my mouth smiling calmly as my voice said, "NO I'm afraid not. Maybe next time."

"I'm sorry we have to have you come down here so often. But hopefully, one of these times we will have the right man for you to identify," the investigator said using his condescending voice.

"It certainly doesn't bother me! I only hope you will be able to find him. We can't let that kind of man be free to hurt someone else," my voice replied while my mouth smiled graciously up at him.

As Mother and I were walking out of the station, she squeezed my hand saying, "You're doing fine Deedy, I'm so very proud of you."

"Thanks, Mother," my voice said as I curled my hidden toes so tightly with each step, that I could feel the skin burn.

Mother was proud of me and constantly let me know. She had been going every place with me since it happened. I imagine she was afraid that awful man would come back. Sometimes when I was with her, I felt so good, so warm and safe. She was the only person I could be with who made me feel that what happened to me was unimportant and that the fact that I was alive was all that mattered. I wished Daddy felt the same way toward me, but I was sure he didn't. His interaction with me had changed, and I didn't feel like I was his 'little girl' now.

More days were marked off on the calendar. Another week that I had no memory of what happened had passed. As I lay on my bed looking at the ceiling, all the bad things left my body. That coldness was gone, along with the choking feeling I got when I tried to talk. No eyes were staring at me, and there were no questions to be answered. I didn't have to laugh when I didn't want to, or play-act and smile if I didn't want to. My room was the only place on earth where everything seemed to be safe and real. Out there, with all those kids and teachers, life was full of miserable sensations. I couldn't relate to all those people in the outside world. My feelings had to be hidden whenever I was outside of my room. And, even though the uncomfortable feelings inside me were overwhelming no one could see them. My room was soft and warm, full of yellow and lavender flowers and a sense of peace filled me with each breath I took.

Suddenly my muscles stiffened when I heard Mother's voice burst into my world, "Deedy, you shouldn't be in your room all by yourself, you shouldn't lay there thinking all the time. The best way to forget is to be with your friends having fun. Susan and Kristin have called you several times, and you haven't called them back yet. Please come downstairs now and call them."

A cold wave swept through me at the thought of having to return to their world. I didn't want to do anything with them. Why couldn't everyone just leave me alone? When I was in my room, I felt so clean; so good; so real, but out there; oh how I hated it out there.

"Okay Mother, I'll be down in a minute," my voice echoed in my head. As I walked downstairs, my body became numb again and unreal. I obligingly returned the phone calls and learned that Susan wanted me to come over to her house to help them wash cars again. She said something about getting back at Jean for the way she drenched us last week. I guess I had been there, even though I had no recollection of the event. What difference did all their silliness make to me?

Every night after I went into my bedroom I heard Mother talking on the phone. She talked about me as though I was some specimen being examined. "She has adjusted so well; we are very proud of her and lucky to have such a well-balanced daughter." Always the same portrayal, always "well balanced," and "well-adjusted." I had even heard her say my teachers had commented on my stability. Stability! They were a bunch of fools; they didn't even know who I was. If only I could stay in my room forever, then they would forget about me altogether. When people talked to me, they thought they knew who they were talking too, but they were wrong. When I was forced to be with people in the outside world I pretended I was really in my bedroom, so they weren't talking to the real me. People lied and didn't understand each other. The only safe place for me was my room.

As I heard Mother's voice drone on and on about her wonderful daughter, I thought about the other day. I had looked into the mirror and saw myself. The person in the mirror was a bad girl and ugly because he had left scars on her body that needed to be hidden from others. The ones on her back were easy to conceal from peering eyes, but the one on the hand caused problems and was so repulsive. I didn't care anymore that people thought I had been raped because that was only an idea and nothing anyone could see. When I had to be with other people I pretended I was someone else, someone who had not been taken away, and I always had a smile on my face to fool them.

That same awful shaking came over me again, as it had so often lately. I curled up holding on to my pillow and tried to think of warm things, such as lying out in the warm sun on the hot sand. I couldn't hear Mother's voice anymore, but only a gentle humming sound coming from somewhere inside my head. I could almost see the sound as it floated by on a waving rainbow.

# Chapter Eight

## Fourteen Years Old

Tomorrow I would be fourteen. Months had passed since that awful man had come, and I didn't think about it much anymore. Summer was here; school was out, and I had great plans with Suzy. She would be sharing the next two months with me, living at my house while her parents were in Europe. We would be sisters. She became my best friend and probably one of the only people who seemed to understand me.

Connie moved back to Santa Monica last year and we were best friends again. But now after that awful man came and Connie's mom forbid her from being any place where I was, I found another best friend. Anger and hurt filled me as I thought about all the things Mother and I had done for Connie and how close I thought we were. She should have told me what her mother had done, but instead, I had to hear it from Susan. Connie never called or said anything to me at school. It was as though I didn't exist or had never known her or been her best friend.

*Deedy one year after*
*she was kidnapped*

Suzy was different and one of the most sophisticated girls I knew. Unlike so many of the kids at school, she never asked me those silly questions. Judy and Kathy flashed through my mind with incredibly nervy questions of what had it been like to be raped and was it terrible. I had no answers for them and could hardly believe they had asked me. When I was with Suzy, I didn't have to play games and pretend to be

41

someone else. I was sure she didn't care if I was raped or not as long as I was alright now; she didn't waste time on stupid questions. She didn't gossip and say mean things about other people. I felt good all day and in control. Ever since I accepted the fact that I probably was raped those awful sensations disappeared. The dizziness and buzzing in my ears and clammy feelings also left, and that awful coldness came only occasionally, like when I was at police line-ups. Once in a while, I thought about those ridiculously naive dreams I used to have about a white wedding dress and some handsome prince. I had been so stupid. Sometimes when I went into my room, I felt like someone was sermonizing about how bad part of me had become. Sometimes it seemed that there were two Deedy's; one was good, and one was bad. The good one was not raped, and someday a prince charming would come to rescue her from all the people who wouldn't let me forget what happened.

For the past week I had stayed out of my room as much as possible, and when I did go in I checked around to make sure there was not two Deedy's. If I got some glimmering that there was, I crawled under my blankets and held on to my pillow, which controlled the shaking and coldness, until I finally fell asleep. When I woke up, there was only one of me.

All those unpleasant thoughts and mixed up feelings would be gone forever as soon as Suzy came to live with me. I would be so busy having fun that there wouldn't be time to look back into ugly memories and confusing thoughts.

*Deedy's home on Tenth Street until she was 15 years old*

Last year Mom and Dad moved us from our old house on Tenth Street to a different home on Twenty-Fifth Street, which was right on the boarder of Santa Monica and Brentwood. I loved our different house and its location, even though it was farther away from the beach. We now had a swimming pool in our backyard and the beach fog usually did not come this far from the ocean which gave me a longer time in the sunshine.

Now that I could spend time in the sun in our new home, I was suspended in that perfect space again, where there was no physical or mental discomfort; nothing to intrude into my world. I felt as if I had left my body and climbed into the private solitude of my mind. I have spent much time in this perfect space this summer and only wished I could find it in my bedroom or floating in the pool in our new home, but there were too many interruptions from Mother.

I learned that this place only existed on the sand at the beach where the hot sun penetrated into the pores of my skin to bake me to a warm golden brown. Laying on the warm sand at the beach I was encased in a large transparent balloon that separated me from all the bodies, noises and roughness out there. Everything was beautiful. Only wonderful sensations filled me. My world was warm and peaceful. I had control. I could hear the noise and voices out there, but they bounced off my transparent balloon and never entered my world. There were no questions to be answered or lies to be told.

If only I could find this at home, instead of all that tumultuous confusion. All summer Mother bugged me with intruding questions about where I had been; where was I going, who I had been with, what I was doing or what I had done. She rarely got the truth, and I hated her for making me lie

Suddenly my skin felt cold. Then I realized the sun was dropping down behind the ocean. Sadness filled me at the thought of losing the wonderful warmth that was here a minute ago. The breeze coming from the ocean was chilling, and ugly goose bumps rose on my skin. When I stood up and left my transparent hiding place, I saw my friends had left. When I looked down at my watch, that awful scar on my hand caught my attention, as it so often did. Suzy told me that no one else ever noticed my scars, but I didn't believe her. Mother said the same thing, but she would say anything to make me feel good. She told me I was beautiful. Both of them were full of lies to pacify me. They must have thought I was a fool. I knew what I was, and it wasn't 'beautiful.'

The breeze turned so cold that I felt it penetrate deep down to my bones. As I put on my blouse and wrapped the towel around my shoulders, I saw Suzy coming back from the hot dog stand with Gary and Susan. I gathered my things together so we could start walking.

Suzy and I crossed the Pacific Coast highway to the other side of the street, then climbed the path dug into the side of the cliff that took us up to the park on top. We crossed Ocean Boulevard to Montana Avenue and started the long 25 block walk to my home. As we walked, we talked about our plans for next Friday night. The many lies I had told Mother echoed in my head like a thunderous vibration. My knotted stomach and tight throat made it hard to breathe. How much I hated her for making me lie and feel guilty. She had pried into my business asking snoopy questions, forcing me to hide the truth. Her "love and concern for me" is what she called it. I wished she didn't "love" me so much, that she was in Europe with Suzy's mom. If she only knew the truth, that love of hers would disappear.

Suzy's voice faintly filtered through my thoughts, "Where do you think they'll take us for dinner?"

"What?"

"Dinner, where do you think they'll take us?" She repeated. "I don't know, where do you think?" I replied.

As Suzy talked on, my mind went back to Mother. If Mother only knew. She thought this would be my first date. The only reason she was letting me go out with Dick was because she and his mom were such good friends. It would be a double date because according to Mother, I was too young to go out on a single date. That's a joke!

By the time Suzy and I reached my house the streetlights had turned on which meant we would be late for dinner and have to listen to a lecture on promptness. Everyone had eaten except us, and my brother was leaving as we walked in the front door. I avoided looking at Ted. The disapproval that I was sure he felt made me want to shrink away. He could see through me; I was positive he knew how much I deceived Mother. He never said anything, but I could feel it. A sense of desperation always forced my eyes to look away whenever he appeared.

# Chapter Nine

# Terrified

Summer was nearly over, and I had not been to the beach for the past two days because of the weather. Winter would come and with it the cold dampness that terrified me. School would soon start, and I would again be imprisoned in those boring classes. As I lay in my soft pink world on my back fearing the future and hating the past, the shaking began to take control of me again with its fierce coldness. Why did rain drops have to come and push the sun away? I pulled the blankets tighter around me, covering my ears to block out that awful sounding rain. Over the summer rain had become a dreaded enemy preventing Suzy and me from going to the beach.

I was barely aware of Suzy as she slept in the bed next to mine. Pressing the blanket into my ears as hard as I could, I made a futile attempt to block out all thoughts. Words kept buzzing inside my brain telling me how bad I was. Words making me believe I had two people inside me. And that I was now the bad one because that man destroyed the good one. The buzzing of those hurtful words repeated over and over again with a torturous stridency in my mind. I couldn't listen to those words again; no more good and bad. That dream of the white wedding dress was torn away from me; no more prince charming; it didn't exist. My head pressed very hard against the mattress with the blankets and pillows held as tightly as possible, but still the words pierced through with images swimming in my head. My muscles were shaking with such force that I was afraid I would wake up Suzy. Ever since that day, that terrible day my life was ruined. Why didn't he kill me? Why did I live? The tears began to pour uncontrollably from my eyes, and I didn't try to hold them back. I knew the battle in my mind would soon be over, and I would be left with that peaceful exhaustion that allowed me to sleep.

When I woke up the next morning, Suzy asked if I had been crying during the night. "Just a little," I answered.

She put her arm around my shoulder, "Don't worry Deedy; everything will be all right."

After Suzy had gone downstairs for breakfast, I studied myself in Mother's full-length mirror. I was thin and very tan. The sun streaked hair was quite long and pretty. I wondered why I could feel the scars so much when they didn't show in the mirror. The sun had covered them. I stepped back and stared for a long time until finally concluding that I wasn't ugly, or bad.

The next couple of days eluded me except for a faint recollection of plans that we made and what we would wear tonight for our dates with Dick and Tray.

I borrowed a dress from Suzy that I had always loved and felt very beautiful when Dick came to pick us up. We went to a very nice expensive restaurant and during dinner laughed so hard we barely had time to eat. Everything Dick, Tray or Suzy said seemed so funny to me that I ended up having a wonderful time. On the drive home, I heard Suzy and Tray giggling and whispering in the back seat as I sat close to Dick while he drove us home. There was a warm tingling sensation deep inside me. As I looked at Dick's strong, handsome face, I felt very powerful, while at the same time helpless and lady-like. The air around me glowed causing a floating sensation as if I was suspended in a cloud.

Dick drove into my driveway, then turned the lights off and pulled the key out. He put his arm around me and my head began to spin. The inside of the car was getting too hot, making it hard for me to breathe.

❧ ❧ ❧ ❧ ❧

The spinning I was in was so intense I was sure I was falling when I saw his greasy mustache coming at me fast, and I screamed. I fought him with all my strength. Scratching his face, the skin felt so thick and tough that I couldn't dig in my nails. It was rubbery and tough. I grabbed his hair and pulled with all my strength, but my hands just slipped away. The harder I fought, the less I could move. He seemed to be tightly holding me down. I tried to kick, but he had my legs held down. I couldn't move my arms either. That awful smell was choking me, and the cold dirt under my face scratched my skin. I was freezing and my body was shaking so violently that I could no longer scream. I wanted to run, but couldn't move. He had me tied down too securely. Then a welcoming blackness took me away.

❧ ❧ ❧ ❧ ❧

Chapter Ten

# Where Am I?

I opened my eyes and saw stark, empty colorlessness surrounding me. There were no sounds, no odors, and no feelings. The only thing that moved were two fuzzy eyes peering down at me. The eyes belonged to a nurse's face topped with a white hat. Her eyes kept staring down at me making me feel as if I was a being examined under a microscope. Then I saw another nurse's face and another, all fuzzily floating around in front of my eyes and staring down at me. I couldn't hear them talking; they were in a haze floating away from me and then back again. I opened my mouth, but when I tried to talk, I only felt a rumbling in my throat. There was no other sound coming from me. I took a deep breath but felt I was not getting oxygen. Those awful 'nurse-faces' kept floating around back and forth. Several of them swirled around me faster, until they become a blur of eyes, white teeth and hats. As terror filled my head pushing me into the maze of nurse-faces, I felt something sharp in my arm, and everything faded into nothingness.

As I floated up out of the haze, I became aware of being tied down on a bed. The course sheets under me were chafing my skin making it raw as I tried to move. My whole body was filled with a terrible fear that I had to escape. I pulled against something that was restraining me. Something held my wrists, arms, thighs, abdomen, chest, and head and was holding me down against the bed so tightly that I had become part of the mattress. I badly wanted to move, to turn around, to turn over and to escape. I pulled and pushed my arms and legs against the restraints until they loosened a little bit. The pressure on my chest grew and made it hard to breathe. No matter how deeply I gasped for air, I just couldn't get enough into my lungs. As I tried to fill them again, something hard was pushed into my mouth, gagging me, while at the same time clamping hands grabbed my head, ankles and arms and pressed hard on my shoulders. My brain exploded inside this vise as an overpowering burst of dizzying colors and sounds blew in my mind and shattered everything inside me. The view from my brain terrified me. A jumbled confusion of vibrant colors was pulsing in my brain spinning in every direction with horribly loud screeching sounds screaming inside my skull trying to get out. I wanted to hold on to something and push the horrible, nightmarish convulsions out of me. I was paralyzed as my thoughts yelled to stop pulling me into a place I couldn't possibly survive. Then there was nothing.

After what must have been an eternity, I awoke and opened my eyes, and felt only panic. When I tried to move, I found I was still tied down in the imprisoning vice. I shut my eyes against those bodiless nurse-faces that were still floating around and I screamed as loud as I possibly could through the strangling terror that was smothering me. A sharp object hit my arm and again I was thrust into nothingness. I don't know how long it had been when consciousness again pushed into my dark world. I was sure I was still a prisoner. Keeping my eyes closed I tried to remember how many times I had awakened only to feel something sharp in my arm that forced me back into darkness. This time, I didn't dare open my eyes because I was sure they would put me back in darkness again. I listened and only heard silence. I continued listening for such a long time that I finally believed that I must be alone. Gradually I opened my lids, almost not daring to look at what might be in front of me. The first thing I saw was a row of bars belonging to a cage that surrounded me. I wasn't tied this time and could move freely on the mattress. There were no faces this time either. I sat up and tried to pull myself over the bars to escape, but found I was too weak. I fell back and floated into another deep darkness. I felt a warm object pushing against my mouth. I spit at it as I opened my eyes. That familiar nurse-face was in front of me again only this time it had a body and voice. My feelings of fear vanished and were replaced with anger. I spit again aiming at that face staring at me. I had so many questions inside my brain bursting to get answered. But I wanted nothing to do with the nurse sitting next to my bed. She represented only awful things to me, imprisonment and confusion. I shut my mouth, locking my teeth together so she couldn't push the spoon in she was lifting toward my mouth. "Now, Deedy you must be hungry. You haven't eaten for quite awhile," her voice pierced the silence. I turned my head away from her, clamping my mouth even tighter. "You've been very sick Deedy, and you must feel weak. I want you to open your mouth and eat this cereal."

I felt tears fill my eyes as I turned toward her and asked, "Where am I? What's the matter with me? Why have you been hurting me?"

She smiled as she touched my forehead saying "You're going to be just fine now Deedy. We haven't meant to hurt you, but there were a few times when you were very difficult and it was necessary to use force to calm you down. If you cooperate with us, we won't have to use force again. Just cooperate and eat this cereal and everything will be fine. I told her I didn't want her to feed me. But she was filling the spoon again, so before she could get the spoon to my mouth I asked her where I was and where my Mother was. "You've been here for some time now, and she had to go home to take care of your brother and Dad."

When I heard her voice, a confusing mixture of anger and emptiness brought a flood of memories to the surface. How could my mother leave me in this awful place where they were so rough? How could she just leave me here and go home? Didn't she know the things they did to me? Didn't she know they kept me tied down and imprisoned? I felt myself getting hot as I angrily asked the nurse "when will she come back?"

"The doctor will be in soon Deedy, and will answer your questions. Now you just eat and you'll feel much better."

I felt paralyzed by my anger at her for avoiding my questions.

My legs began to tremble as I stared at this enemy dressed in a nurse's uniform. I felt a sickening sour liquid come up from my stomach and fill my mouth as the thought flashed through my mind that maybe my mother wouldn't come back. Suddenly I clenched my fist and reached out and hit her arm so hard that the spoon went flying across the room and landed on the floor.

The nurse stood up and in a flat, even tone said, "I have some medicine for you to take now." She held out some pills toward me and said, "take this medicine or I'll have to give it to you in a shot. Do you want a shot?"

"I don't want your pills."

She put her hand on my shoulder saying, "It sounds like you want the shot." I felt so weak and sick to my stomach that I turned my head away from her staring eyes. Looking down at myself, I saw that I had on a white gown that had funny looking mittens at the ends of the arms. I couldn't see my fingers. Then I heard someone scream and felt sweat running down my back. I was cold and hot at the same time.

"If you don't take this medicine, I'll have to give you the shot. Is that what you want?" As she talked she had a fake smile pasted on her face.

"What will it do to me? Will it put me back in the dark place?"

"It will make you feel better," she answered without breaking that fake smile.

"Are you sure?" I asked, knowing all the time that I couldn't trust her, no matter what she said. She continued smiling as though she wanted me to think everything was fine. But I could see through her false expression knowing she was lying, which terrified me. She had a powerful body, like a wrestler's. As I looked at her, I could feel myself starting to shake. The shaking took control of me as though I was connected to a vibrator that I couldn't turn off. Then I felt a sharp thing poke the side of my hip, and I floated away.

I don't know how long I was gone this time, but when I opened my eyes, there was another face staring at me. This face looked kind like it belonged to a nice person. "Well, hello Deedy. You've been asleep for a long time. You must be hungry." There was gentleness in her voice. She seemed like she might be someone I could trust, someone who might help me. Her eyes were very dark brown and had a serene, reassuring look to them.

Sensing I could trust her answers, I eagerly asked, "Where am I? What's wrong with me? Why am I here?"

As soon as she said, "You've had a bad experience which we want to help you understand," the kidnapper flashed through my mind, and I said "he got me again, didn't he?"

"No, Deedy, you **thought** he was there again." Her answer was strange, but I liked her anyway.

"I **know** he was there, I saw him and felt him. I was on a date with Dick when the man came. Did he hurt Dick? Are Suzy and Trey OK?"

"Deedy, that man was not there. It was as if you were having a nightmare that seemed real to you. Dick carried you into the house and your mother called an ambulance which brought you here. This is a hospital."

"I don't want to talk about it. Do I have to?"

She said, "No," then continued, asking, "What would you like to talk about?"

I answered "Nothing." Then I closed my eyes shutting her face out of my thoughts.

A picture of me when I was younger flashed in my mind as I sat in my pink and white bedroom dreaming about a prince charming. He would take me to a wonderland, and we would live happily ever after, just like in story books. I used to believe I would grow up to be a good girl and had saved my virginity for some man I loved, get married and have lots of children. I loved fairy tale stories such as Cinderella and expected to live a life of a special princess. Now I knew my dreams were foolish and it would never happen since that awful man ruined me. How stupid my dreams had been. Real life is nothing like fairy tales. Real life hurts.

I looked at the person sitting beside my bed and was again reassured by her gentle eyes. Maybe she would understand what happened. She looked as if she might. Anger welled up in me as I thought of Mother. She taught me that a girl should save sex for the man she marries, just like Daddy thinks. Daddy said, if you give too much to a man before marriage, he will lose interest in you. They both think virginity is some great, wonderful surprise package that must be saved for marriage. What happens if there was no surprise package to save? Does the girl grow up alone to be a spinster?

"Can I help you, Deedy?" Her gentle voice startled me. I had forgotten she was there. I looked at how little she was and wondered who she was. I bet she doesn't even weigh 100 pounds. Her face was very boney, and she looked as if she was a weak and helpless lady. I again wondered who she was.

"Deedy, can you share your thoughts with me?" She gently asked.

I said, "Who are you? I was just wondering if you are like me? Are you still a virgin or did you give it away?"

She responded, "I'm Dr. Branscom, and I'm here to help you."

"Why did you become a doctor instead of getting married? Why didn't you ever get married?" I asked slowly.

"I am married."

"If you're married why aren't you Mrs. Branscom then?"

"I'm married to Dr. Karl, and I go by the name Dr. Branscom because that's my maiden name and when I earned my medical degree, I was still single. I am very proud of my name and of being a doctor so when I married Dr. Karl, I saw no reason to change my name. "

I had never heard of a woman keeping her maiden name and didn't even know if it was legal.

"Then you're not a virgin either?" I asked.

"No, I'm not," she replied with a warm smile.

"You don't look like a doctor. You look more like someone's mother or like someone in the PTA. My grandmother was a doctor too."

"That's interesting. What kind of doctor was she?"

"She was a surgeon," I answered then quickly changed the subject saying, "Why am I here?"

"Do you remember being with Dick?"

"Yes, we had a great time," I answered hesitantly.

"Do you remember what happened when he brought you home?"

"Well, sort of, not really. I guess that's when he came back. He must have been waiting for me. Why didn't Dick help me get away?"

"That man was not there, Deedy, and Dick did help you. He brought you into your house to your mother and father. In your mind, you imagined he came, but it was not real. It was as if you had a very bad nightmare. Apparently, the kidnapping has been bothering you a lot. Did you ever talk to anyone about it?"

"I know he was there," I told her, "I saw him and I felt him and I smelled him."

"It was a very real experience to you Deedy. We know that. It was just as real as the time you were kidnaped."

Tears filled my eyes as I thought there must not be anyone in the whole world I could trust. She didn't believe me. Why? I had thought she seemed like I could trust her.

"You don't believe me. Why don't you believe me? I was there, and I know he was there again!" I stammered through the tears that were streaming from my eyes.

She took my hand and held it firmly while saying, "The mind can play tricks on people, Deedy. Now it is our job to learn what tricks your mind has played on you."

"I don't believe you." I could barely get my words out, "You weren't there! How can you tell me it wasn't true? You think I'm crazy."

She pressed my hand between both of hers and said, "Deedy, I don't think you're crazy. You are confused. I want to work with you to clear away that confusion."

I was angry again and could feel my muscles tense up as I said, "No! You're the one that's confused! Not me! When's my Mother coming to get me and take me home?"

"Do you want to see her?" I felt my anger turn to hate for Dr. Branscom. "Maybe she can visit you tomorrow. But she won't be taking you home. You will be staying with us so we will have plenty of time to work out all the problems and confusion," she said using that gentle voice that made me hate her more.

# Chapter Eleven

# The Doctor

Dr. Branscom was getting fuzzy in front of me as my anger grew so strong that I wanted to hit her. She began to float away from me just as I reached out to strike her. I could see her mouth moving, but could not hear her voice. Then she started to fade away, and when she no longer seemed real, my anger began to subside. I turned toward the wall and crawled under the blankets.

After hearing her walk out I turned to look around at the room, and the gloom of its empty ugliness only increased the hopelessness I felt. Everything was painted light gray and the floor was ugly gray linoleum. There weren't any pictures on the walls, flowers on the tables, or decorations of any other sort. There wasn't even a rug on the floor. Next to my bed, which was against the wall, was a night table with one drawer in it and nothing on the top. Built into the wall on the other side of the room were two rows of drawers on each side of a plain built-in desk or vanity painted whitish gray. There was no mirror in the room. The third wall had dark windows covered with half-closed blinds. The fourth wall was empty except for the door leading out. The chair Dr. Branscom had been sitting in was pushed in front of the windows, and the only other seating was a bench pushed under what looked like a desk or vanity. It had to be the ugliest, the most depressing room I had ever seen.

I shut my eyes and curled tightly under the blanket, pulling it over my face so I couldn't see anything. I lay there for a very long time, desperately trying to shield myself from everything and everyone when I heard someone come in and tell me to get up so "we" could take a shower. I felt nothing as my body automatically got out of bed and followed the nurse down a long gray corridor and into a big room that had showers along one wall. There were no curtains in front of the showers. She told me to get undressed as she went over to turn on the water. I stood there not wanting to undress in front of her. She walked over to me and stood very close and again told me to undress. I wanted to run and hide but instead found myself untying the strings that secured the gown around me. As I dropped it to the floor exposing my body, an overwhelming sense of shame filled me. I felt totally defenseless under her staring eyes. I quickly rushed to the shower and tried to hide under the stream of water pouring over me. The nurse just stood there, not saying anything, but keeping her eyes glued to me. When I finally stepped out from the water, she handed me a towel. After I awkwardly wiped my uncomfortable body dry, she gave me a funny looking gray and white striped cotton robe to put on. It looked like something a prisoner would wear in jail. She told me to come, so I followed her to my room and was surprised to see folded on my bed were my real clothes. She picked up a pair of peddle pushers, a blouse, and some underwear then handed them to me as she said, "Get dressed." I turned away from her glaring eyes and dressed as quickly as possible. Then she handed me my old shoes.

All the time I hadn't said a single word. She was such a stiff, untouchable person that there was no possible way I could talk to her. She broke the silence saying "My name is Alice, and I'll be with you most of the afternoon." I listened to her words, thinking again of the hopelessness of my situation, as she continued saying "If there is anything you want, please let me know."

"My Mother, when is my Mother coming?" I blurted out.

She said, "Your Mother will be here tomorrow." I felt cold and tired and wished she would leave.

What was I doing in this awful place with these awful people, kept repeating in my mind. I wanted to be back in my pink and white bedroom where it was warm. I walked over to the bed and sat down because my legs were shaking so badly now that I was sure I would fall. I could hear funny sounds far away, like moaning or screaming and yelling. The room began to spin around as the nurse held out a paper cup full of pink liquid and told me to drink it. I did. It tasted good. After a couple of minutes, emptiness returned to my body replacing the shaking with a floating-like warm numbness. With the help of that pink liquid that the nurse gave me several more times, the rest of the day passed by me in a haze.

The next morning I ran to Mother when she came, and I hugged and held on to her until a warm feeling finally filled my body. As she held me tightly, she said, "You look fine Deedy, how do you feel?"

"I just want to go home, please Mother, please! I don't like this place, and I don't like the people here. I'll be good. I promise."

She hugged me tighter saying, "We want you to come home just as soon as possible. You are good and we love you so very much. But you will have to stay here for a while and work things out with Dr. Branscom." I heard her words clearly as they stabbed into my mind, but her voice sounded far away, very far away.

My head was hot and dizzy, and I kept my eyes shut as I said, "But I'm okay Mother, and I'll be good. I promise. If I go home everything will be all right."

"No Deedy, this is the best place for you now. You're with people who will help you get well. At home, we don't know how to help you. Dr. Branscom has the training and knows what's best for your health."

"Will you stay here with me?" I whispered, knowing what her answer would be. When she talked, her voice became cold and stern, and not at all like my Mother's. I pulled away and pushed her roughly as I yelled "I don't need you anyway. I thought you'd help me! Get out of here! I hate you! I hate you!" As I yelled at her, the room became a blur. It became loudly clear to me that there was no one who would help me.

Next, I saw eyes staring, all kinds of eyes and lots of nurse-faces with white hats dancing back and forth amid a stream of bright colors. Nurse-faces came closer examining me as if they were looking for something while many strong hands picked me up, then pushed me down and tied me to a bed. I fought against them as I bit into a hard thing that was shoved into my mouth. I saw Dr. Branscom's face amid the stream of colors and sounds. Her teeth were clenched together and would not come apart. I wanted her to know how awful she was. I wanted her to know that I liked her in the beginning but hated her now. I frantically tried to scream out my thoughts, but they were stuck in my brain. As I looked at her clenched teeth, she did something terrible to my head, which pierced it with screeching sounds and agonizing vibrations. Then my mind burst into a BLACK EXPLOSION.

A couple of weeks later I walked out the front door with a crisp white nurse named Betty, and the brightness of the outside world made me squint. I followed the nurse across the yard toward a picture-book cottage. Everything I saw overwhelmed me with its perfectness. The smooth, velvety green grass was of uniform height, with edges neatly cut along the borders of a very clean walkway. The trees looked as though they were imitations, so evenly shaped with shiny, bug-free rich colored leaves. When I looked at the surrounding landscape, I could not detect a single flaw, and wondered how this image was accomplished. After spending so much time inside that horrible building full of so much distorted ugliness, the freshness of everything I saw outside seemed to come from a dream. I could picture little elves busy at night making this yard perfect, only to disappear when the sun rose. The white paint on the cottage we were walking toward was also perfect without a single smudge or worn spot. It was like a doll's cottage situated on the edge of the property and far enough away from the main buildings that it didn't seem to be part of the rest of the institution. We walked up three wooden steps to the front door and entered a screened in porch, which was full of hanging plants of every shade of green imaginable. There were wicker chairs covered with yellow and green floral pillows that looked like they had been sat on often. I wondered why no one had fluffed up these pillows to make them as perfect as everything else. The floor was covered with a woven wicker rug and had large bugless plants standing in wicker baskets in every corner of the room.

A large wicker and glass table had piles of neatly stacked old, well-read magazines that looked as though they were ready to be thrown out. Next to these magazines were three dirty cigarette butt-filled ashtrays. As I looked at them, I was aware of the stale smelling air penetrating my nostrils. This room was about as different from the rooms back in the main building as could be, and reminded me of my Grandmother's place on the beach in Laguna. I sat down and waited for whatever would happen next. I watched the crisp nurse who brought me into the cottage. She looked as though she had just come from the cleaners with her neatly ironed dress and hat that looked whiter than white against her dark black skin and hair. She was very tiny and only reached my nose when I stood next to her. Her teeth were perfectly straight and very shiny white and her eyes were almost as black as her hair. Everything about her was in place and made her look like a ready-made doll fresh out of a Christmas package. She rang a doorbell that was next to a closed door on the inside wall of the room. The door opened, and Dr. Branscom appeared with a big smile painted on her face. She came over to me, and I could feel my body stiffen with fear.

She took my hands saying, "Come on in Deedy." As I walked into the room, she put her arm around my shoulders. As her body touched mine, it seemed cold and stiff, not unlike the smile painted on her face. She told the nurse to come back for me in an hour as she closed the door behind her. I sat on the only chair in the room that was not covered with papers or magazines. It felt good to sit on a soft chair instead or all the hard ones back in the main building. Dr. Branscom sat in a chair behind an old dark, heavy wood desk that completely dwarfed her with its hugeness. There was a clutter of books, magazines, and papers covering the top of the desk, with one of those big book calendars doctors always have on one corner. I was surprised to see a big metal ashtray on another corner with a smoking cigarette resting in it. She leaned back in a dark leather chair that was so big it looked like it must belong to her father, and puffed on the lit cigarette she picked up. The immenseness of the furniture surrounding her made her look even smaller.

"Well Deedy, you seem to feel better, and the nurses tell me you have been cooperating with them." She smiled as she talked. I didn't say anything. She looked at me for a moment then picked up a pen and wrote something down on the pad of paper that was in front of her. "How do you feel?" She asked.

"Okay." I answered even though nothing was or had been okay. All the things they had done to me were a blur of images all mixed up with each other. I remembered hearing lots of loud voices all talking at the same time, saying things like "outburst" and "jacket" or "so wild." The word "Control" was what I heard the most often, like a stuck record always saying "CONTROL – CONTROL!" There had been pills pushed into my mouth along with something else which was hard and rubbery. There had been needles, sharp ones, which punctured my arm or my hip. I had floated in and out of these voices and faces while my body was always tied to something.

There had been times when my arms were stretched around my body and tied behind my back in such a way that I was left hugging myself. Then there had been that white gown with funny mittens at the ends of the arms which I couldn't get out of. There had been times when I was surrounded by a freezing wetness that buried my bare skin under what must have been ice or snow. I remember shaking so violently that I was sure my insides would come loose. When I tried to get up and escape from freezing to death, a tight rubber blanket-like thing covered the opening of the tub I was locked into and kept me held down. I tried to free myself from all these things by spitting and kicking and screaming or banging my head against anything. But I could never get free, no matter how much effort I spent. When I was in a pillow filled place, there had been a humming noise that buzzed in my brain and was punctured with loud screams. I could throw myself against the walls and floor because they were soft and bouncy. All the places I remembered had a cloud-like emptiness that seemed void of anything hard such as furniture or walls, except the ice place that was of freezing hardness.

"I'm glad you have decided to settle down, Deedy." Dr. Branscom's voice penetrated my memories. I didn't reply. "Have you decided to cooperate with us Deedy?" She asked.

"I have to." My voice quivered when I answered, with a weakness that I didn't realize was there. Then words started pouring out of my mouth without my control. "I don't want to be tied down again. I'll do whatever you want me to do."

"If you can behave and stop fighting us we won't have to put ties on you. But if you continue to fight us again we'll have to control you. Everything we have done has been for your good. We are trying to help you." As she said this, the tight skin across her brow wrinkled and made her look very severe. I didn't reply. "We can work together to solve the problems that have been bothering you. Are you willing to help us?"

"I'll do whatever you want me to do?" I replied with total surrender.

"We want to talk with you about the kidnapping and all the things that have bothered you since it happened. We'll talk about anything that you wish."

How could I tell her the things in my mind? I felt such anger and guilt as I thought about that man, and about all the questions and lies, and about my Mother. The tears were filling my eyes now, and I couldn't control them. I was helpless. I tried to hide my face from Dr. Branscom but was sure she saw what was happening to me.

"I don't have anything to talk about." I replied with an uncontrollably wavering voice.

"How about your school or friends? Your mother said you have many friends who are concerned about you."

"I suppose so."

She leaned over toward the desk and again wrote something down. "Would you like to be with your friends at school now?" She asked.

"Sort of, but not that much."

"Where would you like to be, Deedy?"

I replied with a question, "How long have I been here?"

"You've been here one week."

"I don't remember coming here. What have I been doing the whole time?" My voice was coming out stronger now, as I continued, "Why can't I remember anything? Everything is a blur."

"You've been very sick, Deedy."

"Why don't I remember it?"

"You've had several electroshock treatments and they have temporally dulled your memory."

"What's that? What kind of treatment is that? Was that when I felt so cold?" My voice was finally normal and the tears were not coming now as I questioned her.

"An electroshock treatment helps clear your mind when it has become confused. You were very sick when you came here and in a state of confusion. The shock treatments have helped clear some of the confusion away, and now we hope to clear the rest away by talking."

Again, I asked her if that was what made me feel so cold, and she replied "several times you were so out of control that we had to put you in an ice bath to help you calm down. That's probably what you remember." As she spoke, she sounded so kind and gentle that it was hard to believe that she knew what they had done to me.

"Do I have to go through that again? Do I have to have more shock treatments?" My voice was barely audible to me.

"You will be having several while you are here. They are very helpful in calming down someone who is upset. They will help clear your mind so we can continue to talk calmly and solve the problems that are bothering you."

"I'm afraid of them," I told her. "Can't you put me to sleep or something, so I don't have to know what you're doing?"

"We have been putting you to sleep, Deedy." She said softly. "You don't remember going through the shock treatments, and you have imagined all sorts of mixed things that will clear up soon."

"Are you sure I was put to sleep? What was that thing that was pushed in my mouth? Why do I remember so many awful things?"

"You may not have been completely asleep when the mouth guard was inserted into your mouth before the treatments. But I'm sure you were asleep before the actual treatment."

As I listened to her words, a slight shaking began to take hold of my muscles while I desperately tried to control my thoughts. I just could NOT get "out of control" again. I told her I wouldn't be any more trouble and that I'd try to cooperate as long as they didn't do anything more to me. As she stood up, I felt myself copying her by standing also. Then she walked over to me and put her arm around my shoulder gently saying that she would support and help me get well. I promised myself to cooperate and do what she wanted.

"We'll talk again tomorrow, Deedy, and I'm sure we'll have you back on the road to recovery very soon."

Yesterday was October 13th and Dr. Branscom and I have been talking almost every day for several weeks. I look forward to our talks and feel good when she puts her arm around my shoulder as she does each time she sees me. It's easy to talk to her now, much easier than it was at first. I believe I can trust her too because she has kept her promise to me that I would be asleep before any shock treatments. I was so afraid of them and begged her the second time we talked not to give them to me anymore. She responded saying that I had to have them and promised she'd make sure I was always asleep.

Mother visited me every day except on treatment days. She brought bags of crafts for us to do, which I loved. Sometimes we'd sit in the day room and paint or make things out of clay and Styrofoam. I'm the only patient here who works on crafts. No one else brings them, and sometimes the other patients watch Mother and me.

As I looked out my window and saw Mother coming across the lawn carrying a large bag, I could feel the medicine beginning to take effect. The warm, glowing sensation flowed through me, and I knew that anything that might have bothered me before was unimportant now. The medicine that I liked best was given to me at bedtime before I was supposed to go to sleep. I enjoyed the sensation I felt after taking it so much that I tried to stay awake so that I wouldn't miss the feeling. A few weeks ago when I took the medicine, I would fall right to sleep and miss that floating feeling. But lately, it had become easier to stay awake so that I could float through that wonderful happy sensation. The pills they gave me during the day didn't have the strong floating effect, but they did make me feel happy and not burdened with worries. All those silly worries that I used to have before coming here are gone. When Dr.

Branscom and I talk about the kidnapper and some of the things I used to worry about, it almost seemed as if none of it ever happened because those worries don't exist now. I can handle anything without a problem when I'm taking the medicine they give me. Dr. Branscom said I'll be taking it for a long time, maybe the rest of my life, to maintain what she calls my "stability." She compared me to a diabetic who is required to take insulin when she told Mother and me that I needed the medicine and the shock treatments to help keep my thoughts clear.

As I watched Mother coming closer to the building, the only feelings I was aware of were peaceful, contented ones. I went to meet her at the front door and passed an old lady shuffling her feet against the linoleum floor. As she walked the other direction, she turned her head and looked at me with saliva drooling down her chin. Her crooked grin gave her wrinkled face the blank look of a half-wit. Most of the patents here are much older than I am, and we have nothing to talk about. I don't belong with them because most of them are spaced out. Dr. Branscom said I would soon be out of the building I was in now, which was the most secure one.

When Mother came through the front door, I ran and hugged her, breathing deeply to catch that wonderful warm smell that emanated from her and reminded me of home. We walked down the hall toward the day room and we passed a woman who was talking to herself as though she were two people. First, she would say something and then she would answer herself turning her head from side to side. I looked at Mother, but she didn't seem to notice.

"I can hardly wait to leave this building with all the crazy people." I remarked as another old woman sauntered past us.

"It's too bad there isn't some way these patients could become involved in crafts so they would have something constructive to do with their time." Mother had often voiced this, saying that the patients didn't seem to have any activity to fill their days. She was firmly against inactivity, saying time was too precious to waste, and life was too short to spend even one minute unproductively.

"I've brought some yarn for us to weave into a hanging today, Deedy. I saw this picture in 'House and Gardens' that we can copy, and it will make a lovely wall decoration." She said ignoring my remark.

We walked into the day room and there was only one woman sitting in the corner laughing quietly at something while systematically pulling

62

threads from the hem of her dress.

Just as we sat down and began to take the yarn out of the bag, Mother said she wished there was another location we could work in. This day room was the only place where the patients could smoke or watch television, and it was considered a special privilege that would be taken away from them if they misbehaved.

"Let's go out to the back patio," I said to Mother as the pungent cigarette smoke began to make it hard to breathe. She put the yarn back in the bag without talking and we went out the door toward the patio.

There were a very limited number of places where we could go, only the day room, my room and the patio that was fenced in with six-foot-high walls. As soon as I "graduate" to Building Two, I will have more freedom and we will be allowed to sit on the lawn furniture to make our crafts. Building One is the last building I have to "Graduate" into before I will be released.

As we passed the window in the door of "The Room," I saw a deranged distorted looking face peering out. I heard someone say that the entire room was padded, including the walls and floors. Mother said I had been in there when I first came to Westerly Hospital, but I don't remember.

As we reached the patio and started to empty the bag Mother was holding, the freshness of the cool air caused me to take a slow deep breath, flushing the rancid residue from the day room out of my lungs. Every time I came out of Building Three into the fresh air, I would breathe in as much as I could hold to get rid of that awful feeling I got from the day room. There are so many things I hate about being in Building Three. Since there are no mirrors in what I now view as "my prison" I have no reminders and never think about my appearance. How I look used to be important to me. Hopefully, I'll be released from this "prison" soon. I'm trying to work my way into Building Two by doing everything Dr. Branscom and Mother want me to do. Building Two is a little more normal than Building Three.

One more week passed. I brushed my hair, making sure it was the way I like it. Whenever Mother and Daddy were scheduled to come, I tried to work on my looks because I knew how much it pleased them whenever I made a special effort to look good. Mother brought me colorful hair ribbons last week when I "graduated" into Building Two, and she always commented on how nice I looked when I put my hair in ponytails and tied the ribbons around them. I wished Daddy wouldn't come because he always seemed to be so uncomfortable around me and didn't sound as if he knew what to say. Even though he always hugged me, I didn't know what to say to him either so I usually just talked with Mother while Daddy sat and watched.

When I looked in the mirror again, I was surprised by the darkness of my hair and paleness of my skin now that all my summer tan had disappeared. I checked my watch and took one last look in the mirror pushing back a loose strand of hair, and walked out of my room. I saw Mother and Daddy coming down the corridor carrying a big bunch of flowers and a small box of chocolate candy. Now that I was in Building Two, Mother tried to make sure I always had brightly colored fresh flowers in my room to add a touch of cheerfulness to the otherwise dreary environment. I ran to Mother giving her a big warm hug and then turned to Daddy bestowing on him a rather formal distant hug, which he returned in the same manner. He brought me some of my favorite See's chocolate candy filled with a rich, creamy Bordeaux filling. A slight sense of guilt swept over me briefly when I thought about the hug I had just given him. Our relationship had sure changed since that man came. I no longer felt that I was special to Daddy.

The three of us walked through the beautifully manicured garden, making sure not to step on that green velvet lawn. Mother often remarked on the tremendous amount of attention that must have been put into maintaining the lawn and garden. Mother said she liked my imagination when I told her that I thought little elves came out at night and made everything perfect in the yard, then disappeared when the sun came up.

Mother voiced a thought she often made, saying "It would be nice if the patients could participate in crafts as an activity to occupy them. Perhaps they could even plant and care for some flowers in this beautiful yard." Dear productive Mother, never an idle thought.

After they left, I was anxious to receive my bedtime medication so I could again bask in the pleasurable euphoria it gave me.

One week later, after graduating into the last building, I sat down in Dr. Branscom's office. I felt relaxed as we commented on the tremendous improvement I had made. We had worked on solving so many confusing problems and had come to a few comfortable, satisfactory solutions. I've decided that the kidnapper did not attack me because of who I am or what I am, but because I probably reminded him of someone else, someone who had probably hurt him deeply. He must be a very sick man to attack a young girl the way he had. Dr. Branscom said she hoped he would be apprehended soon so he could receive the medical attention that he so desperately needed. We came to the conclusion that I don't remember being raped because I may have been unconscious. Or that maybe my mind couldn't cope with the memory, so I buried it deeply and may never remember what happened. I shouldn't feel guilty about surviving either because none of it was my fault. It just happened to me because I was there at the time when he came by. It could have been any young girl, and I was just unlucky.

Dr. Branscom treated me as if she believed these were my thoughts when in reality I still thought of that awful investigator who told me about it and asked me if I knew the man. There were some things I didn't tell Dr. Branscom, such as I still wondered if there was something I did wrong, maybe like the investigator said, I didn't scream loud enough or often enough. I knew I was right about the stigma associated with a girl who survived a rape; even though Dr. Branscom said it was a complete distortion to view the victim that way. I wished I could believe what she said was true, but I didn't. Too many impressions made on me over the years were like stumbling blocks that I couldn't seem to climb over. No matter how much I wanted to, or how hard I tried to believe her, I just couldn't get rid of that guilty feeling inside me of being bad.

After the first few weeks of discussions with Dr. Branscom, I realized it would be safer for me if I didn't let her know these thoughts. One time a while back, when I remarked to her that I had a heavy feeling inside me that was a constant reminder of my guilt, I got a strong feeling she was displeased with what I said. I soon learned in order to please her I should appear agreeable to her suggestions and get enthusiastic over the solutions she thought we were finding. Another thing I learned very early in my stay here was that if I seemed restless, discontented or confused, she would increase the use of shock treatments on me. I still hated them and to protect myself from having any extra ones I always tried to please those around me who are in authority, such as the nurses, aides, and doctors. I had done a real good job of building a tough protective wall around all my deepest thoughts and could fool even Dr. Branscom into believing all these months in this awful place I was finally well enough to be released. She had no idea how much anger I still had in me. I had even stopped praying for God's help, believing He either didn't exist or didn't care about me and now it was completely up to me to "fix" myself.

# Chapter Twelve

# Released

After my final release, Mother drove me home and when I opened the front door and walked in, I was overwhelmed by the warm homey smell that greeted me. The reality that I was finally free from that horrible frigid hospital was now a fact. A tremendous sense of relief filled me. At the same time, I was aware of a dark shadow looming in the back of my mind at the thought of facing the world full of people I was sure considered me guilty. I also recently added a new guilt that I hid in the back of my mind; that of having been incarcerated in a mental institution. This thought sent chills down my back and made it hard to breathe. I was sure I was not crazy, but because I had been in a hospital for crazy people, how could I ever convince anyone I was normal.

After pausing for only a brief moment, I walked directly up the stairs from the foyer to my bedroom as though a magnetic force was pulling me. I was relieved to find it was unchanged.

"Are you upstairs, Deedy?" I heard Mother's question but chose to ignore it, as I sat down on my bed among the familiar fuzzy, stuffed animals that covered the white lace bedspread. Just as I was about to lie down, I saw Mother standing in the doorway.

"Are you going to take a nap Deedy?" She asked.

Annoyed by her intrusion, I replied, "I'd like one of the pills now Mother, and then I will rest."

"Let's go down to the kitchen for a snack and I'll give you your medicine. You'll have a couple of hours before dinner to relax" she said.

After having some milk and a piece of toast, I walked back up the stairs anxious for the effects of the pill to fill my body. As I pulled the bedspread back and lay down surrounding myself with my stuffed animals, I became aware of the warm fluid-like feeling that was beginning to flow through my arms and legs that would soon push all the bad thoughts out of my mind. I was home, and everything would work out, I thought to myself as I floated into a nothingness feeling.

The remainder of my first day home went by fast and uneventfully. At the dinner table, no one mentioned anything related to my illness or the hospital. There was a strained quiet that prevailed all through the meal. That night, lying in my bed floating through the medicine-induced cloud that filled my room, I felt strangely disconnected from my family. When I woke up, the morning sun was streaming through the windows brightening the pink floral wallpaper to an intensity that made me shut my eyes again. It was hard to believe that just yesterday I had left Westerly. At the thought of having to return in a couple of weeks for a shock treatment, my muscles tensed with a force I tried to control. At least, I won't have to spend the night there again, I told myself.

The second day home also passed uneventfully while I sunned myself next to the pool in the back yard. The warmth from rays of sun transported me into a dreamy maze of pleasant fragmented images from the past. Pieces of a memory of the time Mother hired a clown to entertain at my birthday party streamed through my thoughts as though I was looking at parts of a movie. We had 30 kids in the back yard that day and so much cake, ice cream, and candy that half of it was still left on the picnic table after the kids had gone. I had felt like a princess dressed in my beautiful white lace pinafore with my hair in French braids and ribbons. It wasn't often that Mother took the extra time while fixing my hair to make French braids but since the day was special, she scheduled her plans to allow time. When she fussed with my hair, I would sit like a statue so as not to distract from the wonderful tickling sensation that ran up and down my back and arms. It was the same feeling I got from listening to someone crinkling newspaper, wrapping paper, or cellophane. At Christmas time when Mother and my brother, Ted, were wrapping gifts, I would just sit there glued to the chair so as not to miss a single sound of paper as goose bumps spread throughout my body. I asked Mother once if she got the same pleasure sensations from these things. "No," she said, it hurt her head when her hair was being fixed, and paper sounds didn't do anything to her. After asking Susan the same question and watching her bewildered reaction, I decided that probably no one else in the entire world felt the same sensations with crinkling paper or could understand. It would be my secret and I wouldn't mention it again to anyone.

I was abruptly brought back to the present when I heard Mother's voice calling me to dinner. I felt resentment as I left the warmth from the sun and went into the house to dress for dinner. I ground my teeth together to try to control the resentment that was now turning into anger at Mother for taking me away from the warm sun which was going to set soon anyway. As I sat down at the dinner table I sensed that Dad and Ted were uncomfortable. It soon became apparent that neither of them knew what to say to me. They again avoided mentioning Westerly, Dr. Branscom, or my illness. I tried to bring the subject up twice, but both times their expressions looked tense as one of them abruptly changed to another topic.

The image of all those crazy people at Westerly filled my mind, and I realized why neither Daddy nor Ted wanted to talk about it. They probably worried about what to say to me. I felt so far apart from everyone except Mother as I sat listening to her trying to keep some conversation going. I wished Bambi was still living with us. But since she had become so old and developed senility Mother had to put her in a place in the valley where there were nurses and doctors who could care for her. I remembered how sad Mother was when she decided she could not care for Bambi any longer at home. The memory of Bambi sent sadness through me. I missed not being able to visit her room and receive her wonderful hugs. Her hugs had always made me feel good.

Now at the dinner table, the unnaturalness of my family's attempt to be natural and relaxed around me only accentuated the distance between us. I suppose they were afraid that something they might say would trigger some craziness in me. I was sure Ted was especially afraid of what I might do since the last time he even saw me was when Dick brought me home in that crazy state of mind. Mother said he didn't visit me at Westerly because of his aversion to sickness and hospitals. As I thought about how much I used to admire Ted, the lump of food in my throat almost gagged me. There was a time long ago when we were close.

I tried not to listen to their voices, as I realized that my experience in Westerly was something that we could never recognize verbally. Maybe it was too embarrassing to them. By the end of the meal, I didn't even try to contribute to the conversation, and it took all my effort to get the food passed the lump in my throat. Immediately after dinner, feeling drained, I told Mother that I was tired and wanted my pill early so I could go to bed.

That night, lying under the blankets, I saw myself as a huge blemish to my family. Mother's behavior toward me hadn't changed, but Dad's and Ted's had, and I felt completely alienated from them. I drifted off to sleep that night without ever enjoying the effects of the medicine. The next few days passed in much the same way. I would be returning to school next week and had hoped it would be different there.

I had another problem facing me now that I was returning to school. After missing almost two and a half months of study and remembering almost nothing about what I had learned in school, I would be horribly behind all of my friends. I was afraid of the huge amount of makeup work I'd have to do, and I was afraid the shock treatments had messed up my memory so badly that my brain would not work. After a shock treatment, I had absolutely no memory. I wasn't even sure of my name or who I was, let alone trying to remember school material. When I shared my worry with Mother, she told me that the teachers would not put too much pressure on me. "All they expect from you is for you to do the best you can," she said trying to reassure me. I knew deep down that it probably wouldn't work and that I would most likely fail to go into the next grade.

Later in the week, Kristin, Suzy, Susan and Karen came over for the first time since I came home. At first, I was uncomfortable and didn't feel like I belonged with them. I had no idea what to say. But Susan was so warm and when she impulsively hugged me saying "Hi, stranger, we sure missed you." I began to relax and felt like maybe I would belong. I responded, with a grateful return hug welcoming the familiarity of my longtime friend. After they had filled me in on all the recent happenings at school, I confided to them that my memory was really bad now and that I was afraid I was going to have problems at school. Kristin said she'd help and even went so far as to commit herself to driving me to and from school now that she had her driver's license. Kristen was a year older than most of us, and her folks gave her an old Ford car for her 16th birthday. I glowed in the warm feeling my friends gave me, and for a few short minutes almost forgot that I'd been away from them for so long. Only once, after I mentioned the word 'Westerly,' did they seem uncomfortable. I immediately sensed that they were embarrassed and promised myself not to make that mistake again. While lying in bed that night basking in the after-glow I felt from the afternoon, my thoughts were happy and full of optimism.

The next morning, I anxiously looked in the mirror one more time before leaving for school with Kristin and was pleased to see such confidence in the expression on the face staring back at me. The emotional turmoil inside me was well concealed. The tranquilizer Mother had given me this morning was doing its job, and I was able to control the fear and shaking I felt inside. After critically examining the image one more time, I decided no one would be able to see the extra weight I had put on at the hospital. The skin was tan again, and the hair was behaving just the way I wanted it too. I held my stomach in as tight as I could and stretched my back straight up with my head high, which added an inch or so to my height and made me look confident. Awhile back when I was learning to hide my feelings from other people, I discovered that when I held my body in this position, everyone thought I was full of confidence. No one bothered me with questions like "are you all right?" Or "are you feeling O.K.?" Those questions always stirred up a furious feeling inside, and I would do almost anything to avoid them.

The front door bell rang, and as I ran down stairs to greet Kristin, I swallowed over and over again trying to choke down the thick throbbing sensation in my throat. As we drove into the parking lot and I saw all the kids walking around, I had to breathe as deeply as I could several times to control the feeling of panic that was rising inside me. Then I closed my eyelids, pressing them tightly against my pupils to clear away the white spots that were forming in front of me. I could feel the warm clamminess under my arms and down my back and wished I had chosen something other than this sweater to wear today. If only I had taken more tranquilizers this morning instead of just one, I thought to myself. Taking a deep breath and straightening my back, I stepped out of the car and closed the door behind me. Kristin and I walked down the hall to my first class, and somehow I managed to ignore the violent turbulence inside that was almost blinding and deafening. As we continued walking, I began to realize that no one was staring at me, that there were no eyes peering in my direction and that this time my return to school was going unnoticed. Gradually, as the turbulence subsided and my breathing came easier, I felt a wave of loneliness sweep over me. Apparently no one even cared if I was here, or maybe they had forgotten me after two months of absence.

We entered my first classroom and Kristin introduced me to the teacher, who said, "If you need any help, Deedy, please just ask me." After Kristin had left the room and I looked around not recognizing any of the faces of my classmates, a sense of fear engulfed me as I realized I was on my own. Each hour of that first day seemed like a year. So many things that I could not remember confronted me that when lunchtime arrived, I was completely discouraged. I didn't see how I would ever be able to catch up with my classes when I could not even remember my multiplication tables or the states of the country or what a noun or a verb was. Evidently those shock treatments had wiped everything out of my brain.

At lunch, I couldn't even remember how much anything cost. On the way home with Kristin, I confided to her about my problems, and she promised to help me. I didn't want her to know how scared and lonely I felt, so I tried to joke around about the 'retard' I'd become. During this confusing time I had not asked God for help because I was sure I was on my own. It would take many more troubled years before I would accept that God had been there for me.

When the teachers realized that I couldn't remember most of the things I'd learned in order to get this far in school, they knew I needed extra help. The various teachers appointed several kids to help me with the class work after they recognized the extent of my memory loss. Even with others helping me I had a lot of trouble concentrating on what I was supposed to learn, and I failed most of the tests I took. The teachers let me take them again and again until I got passing marks. Sometimes I cheated by writing the answers on my arms before the test, but I was never caught. There was a constant battle going on inside me as I tried to hide my awful feelings of isolation. Apparently I was very good at deceiving others, because the kids in my old group were taking for granted that I would return to all the same activities I had been involved in two months ago. I didn't even remember what these activities were, but I soon learned that whenever anything perplexed me, I could hide my confusion if I just kept my mouth shut. Eventually, lots of the mysteries unraveled and the pieces to each puzzle began to fit in my mind.

After the first day, I never again made the same mistake of taking only one tranquilizer in the morning. I made sure there were three of four in my purse each morning before I left for school. The first time I had to sneak the key from Mother's purse flashed through my mind. I remembered how scared I was, even after I had taken the extra pills and put her key back. I was afraid that she might discover some of them were missing when she opened the bottle for the next dose I was supposed to have. I had hidden the pills inside one of my shoes at the bottom of my closet. The only way for her to find out what I had done was if she counted the pills, and I didn't think she would do that. I also worried that when she got the prescription refilled for those pills, the pharmacist would say the prescription couldn't be filled so often. But that didn't seem to happen because there were always more pills when I went to get extras.

One of the biggest challenges I faced during school was when the teachers were showing us how to do something. I had no idea what any teacher was talking about and often didn't even hear their voices while their mouths were moving. I guessed it didn't matter, because somehow I passed the tests, either by copying someone else or by just taking them over and over until I got it right.

It had been three weeks since my return to school, and the most important thing I learned was not to mention the word 'Westerly' or the word 'hospital' or that I was ever sick. The first time when I referred to it, the reactions were the same as my Dad's and brother's. The second time, we were eating lunch when Susan mentioned that Bill was as "nutty as a fruitcake" and "belonged in the Looney bin." After saying that, she turned toward me, her face flushed with embarrassment and said, "Oops, I didn't mean that." Shame filled me as I realized that probably everyone thought of me in connection with crazy people and "Looney Bins." So I said, "He is sort of nutty." I wanted her to know that I could judge strange people too and that she didn't have to worry about what she said around me.

Over four more weeks of school passed very slowly, and I was so glad that Christmas vacation was starting tomorrow. As I walked toward my favorite class and teacher, Mrs. Brown, who was in the art department, anticipation filled me about the Christmas party we were having in her class. A warm, confident feeling filled me at the thought of how wonderful Mrs. Brown was to me. She seemed to think I had a very special talent for painting and always displayed my pictures on the walls. Each day, comforting warmth flowed through me releasing all the tension that had built up during the day. I knew that as soon as I picked up that paint brush, I could climb into the paper and become a part of it. When my work was completed, I couldn't remember painting what was on the paper because the time had gone by so fast that it seemed like a flash. The pictures on the papers were always very bright and usually a combination of yellows, reds, and oranges. Sometimes blue was used, but only if it was a very intense vivid shade. The scenes were usually of people escaping some danger, such as the one that showed kids running out of a burning building. Mrs. Brown often showed the class my paintings to demonstrate some point she was trying to teach the class, especially when it pertained to expression and emotion. She said my pictures were filled with action and feeling. Of all my teachers, she is the only one who seems to think I could create something outstanding. All the other teachers were always protecting me, offering to help me, or just ignoring me. After leaving Mrs. Brown's class, I had such a great feeling and for a while, I could tackle anything.

That night as I lay in bed waiting for the good feeling to start flowing through my arms and legs, I thought about the shock treatment I was going to have the day after tomorrow. I wished there was some way I could convince Dr. Branscom not to give them to me. They caused so much trouble when I returned to school. This would be my second treatment since school started and everything I had learned before my last treatment had been erased from my memory. I had returned to school with no memory of anything I had learned the week before, and I had to spend the entire week relearning everything.

At this rate, I would never graduate from school. Every time I took one step forward the shock treatments put me further back from where I started. If only Dr. Branscom would just give me more medicine I was sure I could "function" quite normally without the treatments. "Function," that is the word she uses as though I was a machine that was supposed to run a certain way. Of course, she doesn't know about all the extra pills I already take, but I'm sure if I had even more "medicine" everyone would realize I don't need the treatments.

Last time during my appointment with Dr. Branscom, she commented on how proud she was of my recovery and that soon she would only be giving me one treatment each month instead of two. In my opinion, our discussions are a waste of time, because we never cover the important things. She doesn't know about the loneliness I feel at school or how the kids and my Dad think of me as "crazy." We still talk about the kidnapping and my thoughts on that, even though she knows that it is no longer important to me. She feels I am making progress because I was elected president of our girls club at school and the kids call me at home all the time. In her mind everything is just fine. The only good thing she did for me was give me the pills. As long as I take them the problems just sort of float past without touching me. I'm afraid if I didn't have them my emotions would show and everything would get messed up again. The pills keep me in harmony with the rest of the world. Thank heavens she said I can continue taking them as long as they help me. Once she told

Mother and me that some patients who have had emotional problems take medicine and have shock treatments the rest of their lives. I don't know if I'll have to do that, but I know I sure do need the pills now.

I was beginning to float on my bed again as I listened to the voices coming from downstairs. Night after night, Mother and Daddy talked about me. Their voices swam by my ears but didn't penetrate into my mind. The feeling was more intense tonight because I took a second pill after Mother gave me one. Now I was floating so high off the bed that my skin wasn't touching anything, and soft colors were streaming past me.

# Chapter Thirteen

# The Car Wash

The next Saturday was a bright, warm sunny day and as I was polishing the last water spots off the front bumper of Kristin's mom's car, I felt Susan tugging on my baby blue sweater and whispering, "there they are. I just knew they'd come." She was looking down the street behind me in the direction of a 1953 green and white Chevy that was slowly coming toward us. "Just wait till you see them, Deedy! They're all so cute! As I listened to her, I continued polishing the chrome bumper so I would appear more interested in my work then in the boys who were in the car as it came to a stop next to me.

Susan had talked me into joining the car wash the girls were having in front of her house to earn money. Several times last week she told me about the darling boys who had stopped to talk while the girls were busy at last Saturday's car wash. She insisted that I help this Saturday so I could see for myself how cute they were. Hesitantly, I had answered that maybe I could find some time to help because I sure could use the money. I ignored her comments about the boys, not wanting to reveal the anxiety the subject of boys caused in me.

I heard the Chevy stop right next to the side of the car where I was wiping the glass on one of the headlights and trying my best to appear casual and uninterested. I moved over to the other headlight trying to seem concerned with a spot I saw while I listened to the flirting that was going on between Susan, Suzy, Peggy and the boys who were sitting in the car with the motor still running.

I felt a sharp jab in my chest when one of the boys said, "Hey Susan, who's your stuck-up friend?" I just knew he was talking about me. "Oh, that's Deedy, and she's not stuck-up. She just likes to work hard," laughed Susan, as I continued to pretend I hadn't noticed them.

"Hey, Deedy." I acted as though I had not heard. "Hey, Deedy if you keep rubbing that light so hard you'll wear a hole right through it." Still I didn't look up at the driver of the car who had spoken, wishing he would disappear.

When I heard the other guys laugh at his remark, I glanced up and then turned back to my work quickly so they would not see how red my face was getting. I was so uncomfortable I pressed my teeth together grinding them against each other and curled my toes tightly against the insides of my shoes, trying desperately not to let anyone know what I felt like. I wanted them to think I had not heard what was said. Suddenly the driver of the Chevy revved up the engine, causing a deafening rumbling roar and I jumped back, dropping the rag from my hand. He slowly drove the car up in front of me, made a U-turn and stopped next to where I was picking up the rag. He revved the engine again several times and drove away down the street in a very cool, confident manner. All the time, the girls were cheering him on with whistles and chants of "go, Freddy, go!" There was no way I could convincingly ignore such a racket any longer, so I casually watched as the car disappeared.

After they had left, I felt relief but regretted having acted like an uninterested outsider. I went inside Susan's house and took one of the pills from my purse and put it into my mouth, swallowing it in a gulp. Then I decided to take another one to be sure I'd get rid of the overpowering emotions inside me. Three more cars full of high school boys cruised by us that afternoon, all making as much commotion as the Chevy driver had made. By the time the third one stopped, I felt light-headed and confident, and aggressively joined in the fun. Soon I realized that these boys must not know anything about my past because they were flirting with me just as much as with the other girls. I began to respond to them and was soon having fun. Up to now I had thought everyone in the entire town knew about me, and I felt such a surge of freedom believing these boys didn't.

At school, all the boys had turned their heads away from my direction whenever I was around like they didn't want to face me. I was never quite sure if they were embarrassed by me because I had been kidnaped, or because I had been in Westerly, or maybe both. No one had ever told me what rumors were spread about me, but I could imagine they were bad. During all the months, I'd been back to school, no boy had come up and talked to me. They didn't tease me or say mean things; they just acted like I wasn't there.

I was feeling so free and proud of myself as the third car drove away. I knew I'd been a hit with those boys. We were emptying the pails of soapy water and rolling the hoses up when the Chevy came back, roaring to a stop at the curb. "Hey, girls, don't fold up shop, we have another car for you," the driver said as he stepped out of the car.

When I saw his face, a tingling sensation started deep in the pit of my stomach and crawled up my back to the base of my neck. My hands were getting warm and clammy, and it was getting hard to breathe as I looked at his eyes. They were beautiful, almost a transparent blue color with flecks of green in them. Over his eyes were thick sandy colored brows that gave a rugged look to the softness of those gentle eyes. His hair was a sandy color and was thick and wavy. When he smiled, the corners of his eyes crinkled up toward his hair, making it look like he was squinting. He had a big smile that showed a row of even white teeth with deeply defined dimples on each side of his mouth. The skin on his face was almost completely covered with soft brownish-red freckles of all sizes, making him appear very tan. I had to turn away from him because I felt ashamed of my thoughts. I was imagining his bare skin touching mine, with his arms around me. I walked toward Susan's house to get away from him. The other boys got out of the car and went up to Susan paying no attention to me.

I busily turned my attention back to rolling the hose up, when I heard his voice very close behind me saying "don't put that away." I was overwhelmingly aware of the feeling of his skin on my hand as it brushed against mine when he took the hose and threw it toward Susan saying "Here, wash my car." "It will cost you one dollar Freddy," Susan yelled back. "That's fine, but do a good job," he replied, turning his attention back to me. His touch almost burned me with a spine-tingling sensation.

I tried not to look at his eyes, even though my focus was on his face as I pressed my toes hard enough against the inside of my shoes to cause a cramp in the arch of one foot. I worked hard at controlling my emotions, not wanting anyone to know what I felt.

"Do you live here?"

I had to force the word "No" out of my mouth.

"Where do you go to school?"

"Lincoln Jr. High," I replied with a little more ease.

"What are you doing after the car wash?" He asked in a voice so warm and gentle that I began to relax.

"Nothing much I guess I'll just go home," I replied when I heard him ask, "How about getting some ice cream with me?"

The tingling returned to the pit of my stomach, and I felt my head spin with a pleasant dizziness.

Then the words "you don't want to go with me" tumbled out of my mouth before I knew they were there. I quickly rephrased my words to "I mean I don't think you want to go with me."

"What do you mean I don't want to go with you? I just asked you to go with me didn't I?" He said looking bewildered.

"I - well - I mean," I stammered, "umm, there is something I think you should know before you go anyplace with me." As I heard my words, I felt anger and confusion at myself for what I was about to tell him. Why did it seem so urgent that he know? It was almost as though there was someone else inside me pushing the words out of my mouth.

"Have you got a boyfriend?" He asked.

"It's nothing like that. It's just something I think you should know about me." Taking a couple of deep breaths and clenching my eyelids shut. "Did-you-ever-hear-about-a-girl-who-was-kidnapped-and-raped-last-year?" The words blurted out so fast that they ran into each other.

He shrugged his shoulders, saying "Ya, I heard something about it, but I don't remember what."

"Well — that was me." I said boldly and then waited for him to take back his invitation. But his only comment was, "That's too bad, but what does that have to do with me?"

I continued as though I was trying hard to discourage him by blurting out, "well-I-was-also-in-the-hospital," as one long word.

"Gee, that's too bad, are you alright now?" He said furring his eyebrows up in the center making him look like he was sincerely concerned.

"I mean – I mean I was in a mental hospital," thinking he might not know what I meant.

"You're OK now aren't you?" He asked.

"Yes," I said feeling foolish.

"I still don't see why I wouldn't want to take you for some ice cream, do you?" He seemed so confident as I looked at his face. I was drawn into those incredible eyes that seemed to reveal a gentle softness hiding behind that rugged beautifully handsome face.

As we drove away I could hear Susan, Suzy and the others shout "boooo" and whistle at us. What a glorious afternoon we had as we talked for hours about everything and anything. Never, had I felt so comfortable with anyone. It seemed as though I had known him forever. We agreed on everything and were able to talk about the dreams and fantasies we both had. At first, I was surprised to learn that he had dreams of beautiful maidens that were very much like the dreams I used to have about some prince charming. All dreamy and fairy-tail like.

That evening after he took me home, I felt so good inside that I didn't even ask Mother for my customary afternoon pill. That night while lying in bed, I floated through a dreamy experience with Freddy, as I envisioned him making love to me. It was so real that I could feel his skin pressing against mine.

# Chapter Fourteen

# The Boy Friend

The next morning, after eating breakfast, I heard the phone ring and knew before picking up the receiver that it was Freddy. He told me he'd be over to pick me up in ten minutes. We spent the day walking barefoot on the empty beach as we held hands and talked some more. I could feel my desires building up to such strong force that I had to stop and sit on the cool, moist sand to regain my composure. As I sat there, I drew pictures in the sand, trying to distract my mind from all the sensations that were flowing through my body. I didn't want Freddy to know what was going on inside me as he sat down so close his arm touched me. Then he reached his arm around my waist and I felt completely powerless to control my emotions. I had to turn away so he wouldn't see what was happening to me. He turned my face toward his and gently brushed his lips against my neck and up to my ear. I felt a feverish warmth flow throughout my body and down my limbs.

Within seconds we were lying down, holding, caressing and kissing each other in a frenzy of insatiable passion. The passion was totally out of control as I experienced my first sexual intercourse. As he drove me home, we talked about how wonderful we felt and how much we cared for each other. We both seemed to feel the same emotions toward each other. The image of him was still vivid in my mind when he had turned to me after our love making. Tears had shown in his eyes as he smiled and clutched my arm, saying "I've been so lonely for such a long time. Deedy you don't know how glad I am that I found you." I asked Freddy if our lovemaking had made him lose respect for me. He reacted to my question by holding me closer and saying "Deedy, we're so close now that I could never lose respect for you. Today we became one."

That evening, when I walked into the house, a strong sense of guilt reappeared and interrupted my wonderful feelings of the day. My mind was so full of thoughts of Freddy that I hardly heard Mother's voice as she asked, "where have you been all day, Deedy?" As I started up to my bedroom, I answered "washing cars at Susan's and the beach."

"You were at the beach?"

"Yes, at the beach," I replied impatiently, feeling angry at her intrusion into my world.

"Who were you with at the beach?" She continued.

"No one you know. Just a boy named Freddy" I answered feeling angrier because her questions were making me feel guilty.

I could hardly believe her when she said, "I don't want you to spend time with one boy alone, Deedy."

I replied, as sarcastically as possible, "What do you think will happen Mother dear? Are you afraid your darling daughter will lose her virginity?"

"It isn't necessary for you to be sarcastic Deedy. You know we have rules in this house, and one of the rules that pertains to you is that you are not permitted to be alone with one boy for any length of time. You know your father and I want you to enjoy the company of many boys until you're older."

As I listened to her words, I realized that I would have to see Freddy without her knowing about it. There was no way I was going to stop seeing him. Nothing she could say or do would stop me. I rushed up to my room and yelled back to her, "Yes dear Mother, anything you wish," feeling anger at her for not understanding me or what I needed.

As I looked in my shoe for my hidden pills, I felt panic rush through me as I saw there was only one left. I swallowed it and rushed into the study, closing the door, to call Freddy on the phone. When I heard his voice, I wanted to be with him so much that I could feel myself shaking.

After closing my eyes and gritting my teeth as hard as I could, I calmed down enough to tell Freddy, "My Mother doesn't want us to see each other. I'll have to sneak out to be with you. I hate her so much. She thinks she owns my entire life. I'm not going to let her come between us. I hope you're OK with us being sneaky. Will you help me?"

His voice filled me with strength as he said, "Yes honey. Nobody can stop us after today. Don't worry. We'll work it out. You remember? I told you that my mom works from 7:30 in the morning and doesn't get home until 6:30 at night. We can spend every afternoon here, and no one will ever know."

"Oh Freddy, I'm so glad you understand. Right now I wish we were together. I don't know how I'll ever be able to wait." After my words poured out I regretted them, fearing my honesty would cause Freddy to lose interest in me. All my life I had heard that a girl should never tell a boyfriend her true feelings. "Never chase him"… "play hard to get"… "don't you ever call him"…"let him call you"… "don't be forward "… "never go all the way" … "he'll lose interest."

Freddy's voice filtered through saying, "Deedy, are you alright?"

"Yes, Freddy. Yes. I was just thinking about today." I lied.

"I'll pick you up in front of the school tomorrow afternoon Deedy. Don't worry. We're going to make this work. We belong together."

After we hung up, I was silent during my meal at the dinner table with my family, after which I went upstairs to bed. Later when I heard the television on, I quietly tip-toed down the stairs and took Mother's key to the medicine cabinet. Feeling relief at my success, I tip-toed back upstairs, tensely clutching the pills safely in my hand.

I went into the bathroom to get a glass of water, and when I looked in the mirror above the basin, I was shocked to see the other face looking at me. I hadn't seen that second person inside me since before going to the hospital and thought she was gone. She didn't say anything; she just stared at me. I turned the light off and stood in the dark for a long time, listening to myself breathe. A choking lump was in my throat, and I wasn't sure if I would be able to swallow the three pills in my hand. It was really important that I get them down because I knew my control was leaving me. That awful shaking was making it hard to stand still and the humming sound in my ears was getting louder. I put the pills on my tongue and forced them down with my throat muscles, almost gagging. I held on to the sink, swallowing the nauseating liquid that had come up in my mouth and waited for the shaking to subside. Finally, after what seemed like an eternity, it left. Next, the humming and dizziness faded along with the image in the mirror. I climbed into bed, pulled the blankets over my head and buried myself as deeply under them as I could. The usual euphoria that came with my nightly pills didn't appear that night. Instead, all I could hear was Deedy's voice telling me that I made a big mistake today and that my prince charming would certainly not ever come. I wanted to scream at her to leave me alone, that all I wanted was to get rid of my terrible prison of loneliness. I was still a good person, and Freddy was my prince charming.

Two weeks later on Friday evening, I walked slowly up the stairs in front of the church. I clenched my fingers so tightly against the palms of my sweating hands that my sharp fingernails dug deeply into the skin. After walking up a few more steps, I turned to look behind me just as Mother drove off in her ugly green Mercury. As soon as her car turned the corner and disappeared behind the buildings across the street, I ran back down the steps and around the block to the alley behind the church where I knew Freddy would be waiting for me in his car. Intense anger filled me, burning my head and pressing on my lungs. Because of Mother we couldn't be with each other openly. We had to hide and lie. She seemed so happy when I had asked if she would drive me to our church for 'teen night.'

I jumped into Freddy's car, sliding across the seat to press myself as close to Freddy as possible. His arm encircled me and I lay my head on his shoulder, feeling the warmth and closeness of his body.

Soon the anger that consumed me a second ago began to subside. Nat 'King' Cole's soft voice was vibrating from the speakers. I closed my eyes, allowing the all too familiar words from his song, 'Too Young', swim soothingly through my mind. The dull ache in my jaw from grinding my teeth together began to leave as the velvety sound filled me with the words, 'they try to tell us we're too young.' The words reminded me of Mother's prying questions. Some day she'll realize that Freddy and I are supposed to be together. We fit perfectly with each other, and we are not too young! Just because I'm "not an adult" as she says, doesn't mean I can't be in love. Her idea that I'm too young to be involved with one boy is stupid!!

I couldn't tell her anything and I hated her for that. I had to hide all my secrets. How could I tell her what I had been doing? She wouldn't understand in a million years. I thought back to the first time I found that ethereal place with Freddy. He told me how very much he loved me and convinced me that it would be all right for us to have sex, especially since I was not a virgin anyway. It was a gloriously warm moment full of tender glowing exchanges. Even now I could feel that wonderful tickling sensation starting deep down inside and flowing through my legs and arms and up to my head, filling it with a soothing mixture of sounds and colors.

With Freddy so close, I began to feel warm and peaceful and was glad I'd taken a couple of extra pills before leaving home. The effect from the medicine was taking hold of me now as my body could feel the vibrations from the speakers. Finally, I was lost in the world around me when suddenly, the warm vibrations stopped. Freddy had turned the motor off and pulled the key out of the ignition. Opening my eyes, I saw that we were parked in a lot beside the coast highway overlooking the ocean. I hardly breathed as we sat in silent stillness for a very long time, afraid that if I spoke, my voice would burst the protective shield that surrounded me. Then I heard Freddy's voice asking if I was OK. When I didn't answer, his arms tightened around me while he again broke the silence with the question, "Are you alright?"

"I'm four days late with my period," I heard my voice coming from somewhere else as my throat tightened making it difficult to fill my lungs with oxygen. The sparkles that had been dancing on the moonlit ocean changed to ugly white spots that blurred my vision.

Freddy's voice broke through my suffocating sensations saying, "Honey, you're not pregnant. Don't worry. You can trust me. I've been very careful."

Not wanting to look at him, I responded by asking, "But, what about the time you didn't use anything?"

"You don't have to worry Deedy. I told you a hundred times I pulled out in time." Silence again engulfed us as he held me, gently rubbing my back with his hands, and soon my body began to relax. We had been making love for over four months, and I knew he had always been very careful.

Because he knew how terrified I was of becoming pregnant, he had gone against his Catholic upbringing by using something he bought at the drug store that he put on himself before we did anything. The memory of that afternoon last month came flooding into my mind with such vividness that I felt like it was happening now. He begged me to let him make love to me without using anything protective. Tears brimmed in his eyes as he said, "I want to feel the inside of you Deedy. Please, I promise to pull out before I come. You won't get pregnant. I promise. Just this one time."

As I lay on the couch in his mom's living room, he kneeled beside me with his head pressed against my stomach. He sounded as if he was crying when he said, "Nothing is going to ruin our relationship. I love you too much Deedy. You've got to trust me."

As I looked down at him, he seemed like a small child. How could I say no when he was so sure of himself, sure everything would be all right.

"Are you positive I won't get pregnant?"

"I promise. I'll pull out in time. I promise! Later, in a few years, I'll make you pregnant. But not now."

Every time we made love, Freddy talked about 'our' future. About how much he wanted his baby inside me. He said it would be our seed of love. Whenever he talked about our future, his mouth would break into a soft smile, making the corners of his eyes wrinkle in such a way that his whole face seemed to smile with happiness. His blue eyes still thrilled me when they were looking my direction. The color was magical the way it sent shivers traveling from my chest down through each leg, making me feel so weak. The color sparkled with life just as the ocean waves do when the sun shines on them. There were times when his beautifully magic eyes filled with tears, and he would say over and over again, "I'm so glad I found you." The first time I heard this, I almost melted with a passion that engulfed me. But as he repeated it time and time again, feelings of fear pushed the good feelings away.

I had not seen any other male cry except my brother when he was younger. I was afraid it might mean that Freddy had a hidden weakness in him that I didn't want to believe could be there. It was important that he be strong, stronger than me. On one occasion after we made love, he poured so much emotion out for me to hear, that I haven't been able to regain the secure feelings I had with him when he first came into my life. I was so sure strong men didn't cry that I felt something was wrong. As I again remembered that day last month when he convinced me that we could safely make love without using anything, I felt the suffocating sensations of fear overwhelm me.

What if he doesn't know as much as he thinks? Maybe he's wrong. My eyes opened and looked at the sparkling ocean waves as they gently rolled toward the sandy beach. As I listened to the soft explosion each wave made when it finally ended its journey to break upon the wet sand, the wonderful times we had over-shadowed the fears that were still lingering deep within me. The months had flown by since we met last summer. Kristin's boyfriend Chuck is Freddy's best friend. Now that Kristin and I are in high school, the four of us are always together. Chuck doesn't have a car, so Freddy drives the four of us everywhere. Kristin has been a great help to me in backing up the lies I have to tell Mother. She's so lucky because her mother works all day, and Kristin has much more freedom than I do.

A coldness settled deep inside when I thought about all the lies Mother forced me to tell. Sometimes I tell so many each day that reality gets all confused with my lies. There are times when my lies seem to be the truth, and other times when they are only part of a dream. Sometimes I get so scared that I might get the truth and my lies confused and say the wrong thing. I try not to even talk to Mother just so I don't screw up. Mother can't know what I do. She thinks I spend two evenings each week with the teenage group at church and has no idea of the hours Freddy and I are together. She doesn't know that he picks me up at the bus stop in the morning and drives me to school, or that we go to the apartment where he lives with his mom for at least an hour several days after school each week.

All those weekend nights that she thinks I've spent with Kristin, I've been with Freddy. Kristin understands how important it is for Freddy and me to be together since she feels the same way about Chuck. She has become my very best friend and helps me keep my secrets.

As I listened to the soothing sounds of the ocean waves, the image of Mother intruded into my mind again, causing an intensely hot anger to well up in me. Because of her, we have to lie and hide the beautiful feelings we share with each other. "Too young," that's all she ever says. "You're too young to spend all your time with only one boy. You need to meet many different boys before you decide on one boyfriend."

Too young - too young! The problem with her is that she is too old. She has no understanding of what it's like to feel the beautiful sensations that come from being in love. I'm sure the last time she and Daddy made love was when I was conceived.

"What's the matter with you tonight Deedy?" Freddy's voice pierced my thoughts and made me aware of the dull ache that had returned to my jaw as I clenched my teeth tightly together. Suddenly the night coldness made me shiver as the image of Mother again filled my head.

"It's Mother. I was thinking of all the lies she forces me to tell. I hate her so much." The words tumbled out as my body began to shake. The shaking became so steady and strong that I wished Freddy wasn't there to see me losing control.

I needed more medicine, but Freddy couldn't see me take it. He pressed me against his body, patting and rubbing my hair as though I was a pet. I felt stiff and rigid, cold and distant from Freddy's touch. I was outside looking in. Control – get control Deedy. Determined to regain my lost control, I pressed my toes against the insides of my shoes. I tensed the insides of my body with such force that it felt like I was pushing against my skin. I concentrated so hard trying to stop the shaking that the sparkling spots that were dancing in front of my eyes became a blur of white.

"Relax honey. In a few years we'll be married and then it will be all over. You won't have to lie ever again." He gently kissed my forehead and then moved to each eyelid pressing his lips against my skin ever so softly. I could feel his warm breath as he finally brought his lips to rest against mine. There was no passion in this kiss of his, only a warm reassurance that flowed into me finally filling me with a sense of calm that pushed the shaking from my body.

It seemed like such a short time had passed when he pulled back saying "I have to get you back to the church now. Your mother will be there soon."

Standing on the church steps, I watched Freddy's car fade into the distance and turned my thoughts to what story I would tell Mother tonight about what we did at the church meeting. As the image of the church group filled my mind, I wasn't sure if I had actually been with them and not with Freddy. Maybe, the memory of being with Freddy was what I had made up. Sometimes, after I was at home the memories of being with him were not as real as my stories.

During this time of intense deception, it never crossed my mind that God was probably watching what I was doing.

That night I lay in bed for the longest time waiting for the floating cloud to carry me away. As I lay waiting, my bed seemed to be filled with a million lumps and wrinkles. The cotton nightgown that I tried to smooth felt like thick, scratchy canvas and my pillow was rough and prickly against my face. The medicine wasn't working the way it should. I had to wait an eternity to feel good. As I waited and waited and waited, anger began to fill me. I was angry at my bed. Angry at the medicine. Angry at myself. Angry at mother. The medicine, why didn't it work? I was already taking ten extra pills before bed. How many more did I have to take? I sat up on the edge of the bed and put my feet on the rug covered floor, I knew the rug beneath my feet was of a soft texture, but it felt like it was made up of tiny pebbles. I quietly tiptoed across the rock and pebble covered floor to my closet where I kept the extra medicine. When I reached into my shoe and found only two capsules left, a wave of panic rushed through me as I realized how often I had to fill it and how fast it emptied. The shoe blurred in front of my eyes, and a tremendous throbbing pounded in my throat as someone's voice whispered "what if you have to keep taking more to feel good? What if someone finds out? Your mother will find out!"

I pushed the two capsules into my mouth, gagging as I swallowed them dry as fast as possible. I sat stiffly on the rock and pebbled floor squeezing my eyes shut, trying to force the panic out of me. Panic was my enemy; it caused me to lose control.

No! I can't lose control. Don't let it happen. Control. Take control. As I rigidly sat tensing my muscles as tightly as possible, I saw the panic that invaded my body as it was being squeezed out from my center and flowing down my arms and legs and out through my fingertips and toes. I concentrated on the panic, watching it travel from me and across the room toward the door. It was an ugly cold glob of dirty gray-brown color that looked at me and screamed a shrill sounding "CONTROL" over and over again until it finally faded through the door. I must have sat on the floor in front of my closet for hours after it left, just enjoying the feeling of being empty. Nothing concerned me. No worries. No confusion. I was beautiful. I was good.

When the chilly night air began to penetrate the emptiness, I crawled back into bed and buried myself under the warmth of my blankets. The bed had a soft, smooth surface which helped me drift on my cloud when suddenly I heard an intruding voice ask me how I would feel in the morning. The mornings had become awful since I had been increasing the amount of medicine I took at bedtime. I was reminded of the heavy, wet, weak feelings and of how I could barely lift myself out of the bed and dress for school. I pushed her voice out of my head with my pillow and reached for the cloud that was floating by.

I woke up the next morning to the annoying sound of my alarm. Turning it off and the radio on, I lay back down hoping the drained, weak feelings caused by last night's medicine would soon leave. The words from 'Rudolph the Red-Nosed Reindeer' were coming from my radio and reminded me Christmas would be here soon. It was supposed to be a beautiful time of the year when all people everywhere stopped whatever they were doing to get together with other people to proclaim a celebration. Mother would never let us start talking seriously about Christmas until Thanksgiving was over and done with. She said three weeks was long enough time to get ready. She said consumers were reminded of Christmas earlier each year because the stores were taking advantage of the occasion to sell more junk to the poor suckers in the world who had no self-control. She would not be one of the suckers. Although Mother had a firm rule that we were never to put the tree up until two weeks before Christmas day and must take it down before the New Year rolled in, she still made more of the occasion than any of my friends' parents.

# Chapter Fifteen

# Christmas Memories

My thoughts went back to Christmases we had years ago. Mother has always had so many decorations that they fill several dozen cartons that were stored in the basement the other twelve months of the year.

❧❧❧❧❧

It was my brother's and my father's job each year to go down the narrow, steep steps to the dark, dank basement and retrieve the many dusty boxes that had carefully protected each precious item. After this was accomplished, each member of our family would pour over the items as though they were looking through some long-forgotten scrapbook full of special mementos.

"Oh, do you remember this one? It was always my favorite."

"The red glass cones, look at how delicate they are."

"The beautiful manger is so old. Do you know we've had it in the family for more than thirty years?"

"The reindeer, you know the ones I mean, the hand-blown glass ones, where are they?"

"I put them in a special place, with the good china. I'll get them later. They've always been very special to me. They are so very fragile and could easily break."

After reminiscing for a while, Daddy brought in the tree we had picked out at the Christmas tree lot. He set it up in the living room while the rest of us stood back to tell him if it was leaning too much in one direction until it finally met with our approval. Next came the major job of the season which was shared by Mother, Ted and me while Daddy sat with Bambi on the couch watching. The three of us always decorated the tree knowing just how it should be done. Certain items went to the highest parts of the tree by Ted because he was tall enough to reach the top, so they wouldn't get broken. We worked our way down to the bottom of the tree, saving the most special decorations for the last step. We took three or four hours to complete the decorating, and when we finished Daddy would plug in the tree lights and then turn off the room lights and the moment of truth would arrive. The three of us stood back and year after year came to the same conclusion. "This is the most beautiful tree we've ever decorated."

Daddy never helped with the decorations, saying we did a better job. Bambi couldn't help because she was very old. Rheumatism in her bones made her fingers bent, twisted and lumpy and she used a cane to walk. I remember a long time ago I used to sit on her lap while she read stories to me. Whenever we visited her in Laguna Beach during the summer she took long walks with me on the beach. I felt sad that she changed so much, but I loved her anyway.

As long as I could remember, each Christmas had been the same, until this year. Christmas day was so close and I became increasingly aware that something was missing. I had no sense of the familiar warmth that I associated with this time of year. The anticipation was absent. I wasn't even sure what to look forward too. Memories of past Christmases flooded over me as I lay in bed remembering myself as a little girl. The excitement of Christmas was something that could hardly be controlled. It filled me so full that I could think of nothing else. I used to sit in school when I was five or six and think of nothing but the tree and what magical packages would appear under it. The Christmas memory that loomed larger than any other occurred when I was about six years old. I could see myself as a little girl in the first grade at Roosevelt grammar school and everyone, absolutely everyone, said there was no Santa Clause. But my best friend Cheri, who lived next door, and I knew different and no matter what the rest of the kids said, they couldn't convince us that he was make-believe. The saddest part was the seed of doubt had been planted and try as I might, I couldn't get it out of my mind. The picture of that Christmas was very vivid. I remembered the day shortly before vacation when I had walked home from school with tears spilling from my eyes as I ran into the house shouting, "Mama is Santa Clause real? The kids all say he's make-believe."

"What do you think Deedy?" Mother asked. I was a naive, vulnerable little girl who wore bows in my long blond hair and so willed and wanted to believe. When I was very little I believed that fairy-tales existed in the real world and were full of beauty and happiness. Her huge innocent brown eyes looked up into the eyes of my Mother, who I was sure knew everything. I held my breath waiting to hear if she would burst the balloon of beauty or restore faith in all that was right?

Mother hugged me and didn't say anything. She didn't confirm or deny the seed of doubt that was planted and was growing roots that would later come back to bear the fruit of deceit.

"NO ... I WANT Santa to be REAL. Cheri and I don't believe those kids at school!!!!"

When Christmas morning finally arrived that year so long ago the little girl, whose feelings I could still feel, was hoping she would be vindicated. She crept down the stairs long before anyone else in the house was aware that the new day was about to arrive in all its glory. The sun was preparing its radiant colors of red and yellow to shine on all the celebrating people below. I felt as if I had become that little girl again. My hair was a tangled mess which indicated I had spent many restless hours waiting and wondering. With anticipation, I quietly spied on each and every item that was under the tree looking for the watch that I had asked Santa to give me on Christmas Day. I stood still next to the gaily decorated tree whose size dominated the room and emphasized my smallness. I deeply wanted to believe, but slowly lost any warmth that might remain within my small body. The emptiness was replaced with the sad heaviness of disappointment. The only warmth that remained in the room came from the tears which silently rolled down my soft pink cheeks. The watch was not there.

The terrible realization that Santa Clause WAS make-believe hit me. He was not real. He was just some elaborate fantasy mothers and fathers propagated. Why? Why would they do such a thing? Thinking back on that day, I felt anger and confusion. Why on this day, when Jesus Christ was supposed to be born to save us from our sins, did parents lie? Maybe everything was make-believe. Maybe Jesus Christ was also make-believe. Maybe mothers and fathers of long ago made up an elaborate story so that they could celebrate something. I sat down with my legs crossed at the ankles and waited. Waited in silence for the others to wake up and join me in the celebration of Christ's birth. Truth didn't exist. The glory of Christ saving us from sin. Was that also a lie? I waited and waited. I did not move and did not cry. I just sat and waited with big brown eyes that were not so innocent anymore. I waited and the seed of doubt sprouted into a full grown cloud. I knew now that everything wasn't what people said it was. Some things were only make-believe.

The sun had risen and shone over the house that was celebrating Christmas. As the morning progressed, and everyone had opened the brightly colored packages that had been decorated with painstaking thought and love, the watch never appeared. I knew now for sure that Santa Clause was make-believe. The kids at school were right. I was wrong and Cheri was wrong. The doorbell rang and Mother answered it and called out to tell me that someone was there to see me. I slowly walked to where Mother was standing.

I could feel myself watching my feet as I walked to the door, my eyes focused down as each foot moved ahead of the other one. I stopped when suddenly a pair of shiny black boots filled the space where my focus was directed. Slowly my eyes moved up to see a pair of baggy red pants, then a shiny gold buckle that securely fastened a thick black belt around the middle of a large red coat. As I kept looking up I saw a long white beard that framed the mouth and rosy cheeks on the face of Santa Clause. I looked up into his blue eyes and my heart dropped out of me. My breath would not come. He was real after all! He wasn't make-believe! I could hardly hear the words that came from his mouth, but somehow the message was received.

"After I'd dropped all the gifts off at all the children's houses last night, I noticed that I forgot to leave something at your house Deedy." He even knew my name. "Here you are, honey. Here is the watch you wrote and told me you wanted."

SANTA IS REAL! The door closed and he disappeared. As fast as my little legs could carry me, I ran to the phone to call Cheri and tell her the kids were wrong. We were right. I was overflowing with my wonderful knowledge. Cheri answered the phone and I told her "We were right. Santa is real. He came here and gave me the watch I asked for and he even knew my name." She responded saying "I know. He was just here and left that doll I asked for." Her voice barely penetrated my inflated sense of happiness.

That was so many years ago. And I still remembered the joy when the little girl had been vindicated. Her sense of truth was restored. Everything was in its proper place and she was very happy. She truly loved her parents and the tree and all the gifts she had received. Christmas was the best time of the year. Looking back on that Christmas, I try to remember when I actually did find out the truth, but cannot. Maybe it just seeped into me. Maybe after the kids insisted year after year, I finally was forced to stop believing. Maybe Santa Clause didn't appear the next year. I don't know how or when I found out. There was absolutely no lingering memory of discovering the truth. The one thing I do know though is that I will be very careful and never fill my children with the same lie that my head had been filled with. What a long time ago that happened and so much has gone on since then.

Christmas Day was almost here as I walked down the stairs to breakfast, my brother's eyes looked through me as he passed by on his way up. I quickly turned to avoid their knowledgeable look. Since he'd been away at college, I didn't have to confront those knowing eyes very often. He's home now on Christmas vacation and only comes home every other weekend, and somehow I could usually manage to be somewhere else. We seldom spoke to each other. We had nothing to say. I knew that he knows about me. I knew he knows about my medicine and about Freddy and my lies. I was sure my brother knew way too much so I was very careful to stay as far away from him as possible. His knowledge was dangerous to me. If he decided to tell Mother about me, my world would crumble. But luckily for me, he seemed to have interests that were more important to him than me. He studied all the time. He once told me he was going to grow up to be successful and rich. He would have all the material things he ever wanted and be powerful and important. We used to talk before that horrible man came and change everything

# Chapter Sixteen

# Family

A long ago memory of sitting on the playroom floor fixing my doll house just the way it was supposed to be fixed flashed through my mind. I told Ted, "No. I don't want to play movie star." Ted was a lot older than me, and I looked up to him because he knew everything about everything. He was going to be involved in making movies when he grew up and was constantly reading magazines that told him all about movie people. I found them boring but listened patiently as he would describe what each famous person did.

Sometimes he wanted to pretend he was a famous entertainer and would ask me to perform with him. I remembered the green curtains in our old house that hung from the archway dividing the dining room from the living mom were pulled shut as Ted fixed the setting for the show.

※ ※ ※ ※ ※

We were Gene Kelley and Debbie Reynolds and were getting ready to dance and sing to the record, 'Singing in the Rain.' Ted knew everything there was to know about putting on Broadway shows, so he made all the decisions.

*My brother and me at the time we performed "Singing in the Rain" for our parents and neighbors. My brother was 6 or 7 and I was about 3 or 4.*

I just followed his direction, standing where he told me to stand and dancing the way he said to dance. We were both holding rain umbrellas that were of a dark silky fabric and shielded us from the rain that you could hear in the background. Ted was very talented and could easily do all the jobs that were necessary to produce a successful Broadway production. He was the stage manager, the choreographer, the music director, the costume director and designer and the producer along with being the talented tap-dancing and singing star of each and every show that was brought to the audience in our home. Mother and Daddy sat in the front row and sometimes neighbors were invited to our gala production and sat with them. The chairs they sat on were folded away after the curtain was drawn shut at the end of a performance and stored, waiting until the opening date of our next performance. We always had rave reviews because the audience was always impressed with our talent. The music was very popular, and the dancing was extremely creative. The glitter and shine of opening night was always filled with a sense of excitement and we, the performers, always had butterflies in the pits of our stomachs. I always dutifully followed my brother's direction even though performing was the last thing on earth I wanted to do.

Playing with my doll house, making it neat and orderly, or serving tea with my miniaturized tea set was much more fun. In those days so long ago, because I admired and loved my big brother so much, I would never have denied him his request to perform with him. I wanted to please him and always felt so good when he would tell me I had done my part just right. Receiving a compliment from Ted was like being awarded a prize. He didn't bestow many compliments and when I did earn one my sense of self-importance was almost embarrassing. I would lower my head and look down with a humility that hid the self-importance that I felt.

Times had changed, and Ted and I had lost our partnership somewhere along the way. We had nothing to talk about now and nothing to share. He was becoming prepared to shake the world with success, and I was left behind to hide my shame alone. He knew about my shame but did not verbally acknowledge it. Only his eyes gave him away. Only his avoidance of me and my unscrupulousness, gave him away. So I stayed away from him too, away from his dangerous knowledge. Now that Christmas vacation had arrived, we were thrown together more than I wanted and I tried my best to avoid him. Wouldn't it be nice to have a brother who would protect me? Wouldn't it be nice if I could go to him for understanding instead of Freddy? It would be wonderful if I could have a brother who would listen and help me. Someone I could tell the truth to. Someone who wanted to be as close as glue to me, yet at the same time someone who wouldn't want to sleep with me. Someone who could understand that I was a good girl, not someone who would tell me to lie down so he could enter into me time and time again.

The Christmas morning of 1956 arrived. I was fifteen years old and full of deception and anger. The family sat around the tree in a group and carefully opened each gift that had been so carefully wrapped. Everything was done with care at Christmas time. The proper "Thank you" and "It's just what I always wanted" said at just the right moment in an effort to please each other. The best part of Christmas morning for me was listening to the wrapping paper crinkle and giving me goose bumps. I would just sit still listing and not saying anything.

Freddy stopped by later in the day careful not to interrupt our family morning together. We exchanged the gifts we had carefully chosen in hopes of pleasing each other. He gave me three record albums that spoke of his love for me, and I gave him the pair of Argyle socks I had carefully knitted for him. He left at just the right time so he would not be late for the Christmas dinner he was going to eat with his mother at his aunt's house. We did not exchange any Christmas kisses, carefully considering my parents feelings. It would upset Christmas day if they got as much as a glimpse of our intimate relationship. So we were very careful not to reveal anything that might get us into trouble.

As the day continued the house filled up with tantalizing aromas that filtered through each room and reminded us that Christmas dinner was cooking. I felt alone and empty. Daddy was sitting in his customary chair watching the elaborately produced Christmas special that was coming from the television set. I was sitting as far away as possible from everyone in the uncomfortably hard chair that no one else ever sat on. As I looked over at my father, I could remember sitting next to him while he warmly put his left arm around my shoulder. The memory made me feel sad. That awful man had taken Daddy away from me. He stole my virginity and with it, he took Daddy away. He said I was his princess, but in truth, I was not even here. After thinking about the past for the longest time, I could face my family no more and ran upstairs to my palace of pink.

"What's the matter Deedy?" Daddy's voice followed me upstairs. I wasn't able to answer as I lay on my bed staring up at the ceiling.

"Deedy, come down and help Ted set the table." It was Mother calling me. She wanted me to join in the merrymaking of Christmas.

Running to the closet, I reached into my shoe and retrieved two pills, one to help me celebrate, and one to help me escape. With a ghost-like slowness, I walked downstairs to join the others on this "happy" Christmas day. There was no sense of excitement within my body. No happiness. No warmth. No celebration. The only feelings inside me were emptiness and numbness. The table was set and we sat down to feast, but before lifting our forks, we thanked the Lord for this day and for the food and for our family. As I heard Daddy lead us in prayer with his deep voice letting God know how thankful we were, I felt like I wasn't there. I was only an observer. When the forks were finally lifted, I watched from my floating spot somewhere above everyone else.

I was somewhere high up near the ceiling in my weightless state. My body sat at the table across from Ted with Daddy at the head of the table to my right and Mother sat at the other end of the table across from Daddy. The table was dressed up in the best heirloom lace tablecloth the family owned with the ancient family silverware and spotless antique china and crystal placed neatly on top of the lace. The three hand-blown reindeer that were never used for anything other than Christmas dinner were carefully placed on a small mirror in the center of the table. Small fiberglass snowflakes and tiny fake trees were strategically placed to make it look like a winter scene. This was the only table decoration I had ever seen at the Christmas dinner table. It was the only one worthy of our admiration. It had been used year after year and then carefully rewrapped in newspaper to save for the next year's ritual feast of Roast beef and Yorkshire Pudding.

As I watched from my transparent place at the ceiling and saw the hypocrisy of this dinner, I felt only emptiness. I knew that this celebration that was taking place for and by those people below me was only a ritual in disguise. It was being performed for the purpose of hiding any rift that might be starting, any breach of family contract, to bind people who are supposed to be bound to each other in a contract of loyalty and love. I could feel my feelings of wanting to honor our family contract. But no one knew what I was really thinking. Repeated rituals are supposed to make the most of the bonding of family love. Family bonding and love ties people together since they live in the same house, or because their grandparents lived together, or because their great, great, great, great grandparents slept together.

Will Freddy and I have celebrations? Will we perform these same acts?

I told myself, "Love your family because they are my family." Mother hugs me and wipes the tears away and my daddy calls me princess and hugs my Mother. He also brings home the paychecks and hands out money. Honor bound to love. We celebrate together. We celebrate that we are a family. The performance was a ritual. It is performed over and over and over again for the purpose of binding one another together in a time of danger. It's the danger from the enemy of gossiping, against those who attempt to penetrate the family unity, against anyone who is mean to us. Why didn't our family bonding protect me? Neither God nor any of my family saved me from that horrible man who ruined everything. But, as I floated in my ghost-like state, I wondered who am I bound to? Who knows me and who is bound to me? I was familiar with the family rituals that were repeated and repeated. It is a ritual to decorate a tree that has been carefully chosen to resemble the one decorated last year as closely as possible, which resembled the one the year before as closely as possible. Repeat. Repeat the same menu that was feasted upon last year as closely as possible. Try not to deviate from anything that has been tried and proven a success. Repeat the same activities that your parents repeated, that their parents repeated, and so on and so on forever, if possible. So what if the neighbors opened their presents the night before? That was definitely not the way to celebrate our very special occasion. The ritual states that last Christmas the gifts were opened on Christmas morning. Therefore, this year we must do the same. Rituals are formal and make people sit straight. Eat with the correct fork. Politely wipe your mouth with the pure white napkin that rests politely on your lap after filling your stomach to the fullest. It makes women slave hour after hour preparing roast beef and Yorkshire pudding so the family can sit together and feast on the "Best Christmas Dinner ever."

All this was done in the name of love. Family love. Looking down from my special place, from my special vantage point, I could see only forced ritual, mindless ritual. Something that someone thinks will cement each and every family member together with loyalty to each other. When the ritual is over and life again returns, will each member remember the lingering aroma? Will the cement of this ritual reinforce the nest; will it remind each of where their loyalties lie? This was the same celebration. The same ritual I had witnessed for over fifteen years. The same celebration that made me feel warm inside, the same one that used to make me feel loved. Is this really the same one? What happened to the feelings? Where did the warmth go? Did that man wipe everything away so easily? Mother was smiling and thanking Dad for the compliment on her dinner, "The best one ever." Ted was filling his plate with his third helping of Yorkshire pudding that was so generously floating in roast beef juice, and I was sitting there completely misunderstood and alone. I had no one to express my desires to, nor to tell the truth too. Only lies. That night the kitchen was hot, and the chore of cleaning up was torturous. The amount of items used to perform the celebration of Christmas staggered my mind. How could so few people use so many dishes, dirty up so many items? But I couldn't let anyone know that I was feeling tortured because the cleaning up of Christmas dinner dishes was also part of our ritual and was performed by the women and children of the house. It usually took about an hour and was accomplished with an attitude of merry satisfaction.

❧❧❧❧❧

That night I broke my Mother's very best Wedgewood platter, which had been used for countless Christmas celebrations without so much as receiving a crack before tonight. As it loudly crashed to the floor breaking into thousands of un-repairable pieces, a cry of total devastation came from my mouth. "I'm sorry Mama. I'm so sorry," I whispered through a torrent of tears. I had ruined the celebration. I alone had done what no one for ever had done. I had managed to destroy part of the family celebration. I alone. How could I be so clumsy? So stupid?

"Oh, Mama, I'm so sorry," I said bending over and trying with all my might to fit each piece back into its proper place. Try as I would, none of the pieces fit each other.

She pulled me up from the floor and held my shivering body in the protection of her arms. She patted my hair and hugged me tighter.

"Deedy, it's alright. It was an accident. It was only a dish. Darling, don't feel so bad, we have others. It isn't the end of the world."

"Oh Mama, I'm so sorry. I didn't mean to. Honest. I'm sorry." I felt my sobs as they racked my soul. Mother didn't know that I was not only saying that I was sorry I broke the platter. I couldn't tell her that I was also sorry I had broken the family bonding of love. I was sorry I lied all the time. I was sorry I was taken away and raped. I was sorry I was a bad person. I was sorry I slept with Freddy. My burden of guilt overpowered me as my body began to shake uncontrollably.

Mother asked Ted to get my medicine as she helped me up the stairs and said, "Darling, you're just tired. That platter wasn't important. It was just an old dish, nothing more." As we reached my flowered sanctuary, she said, "Now put on your nightgown and I'll go down and make you some nice warm milk. You get into bed, and I'll be right back in just a minute."

I was crawling under the covers when Ted came into the room carrying a glass of water and my medicine. He said, "Mom wants you to take this." I dared to look up at him through my swollen and tear filled eyes to see compassion in his expression. But he knows. I'm sure he knows, and he must hate me. As I again looked at his face, it looked as though he might start to cry too. Taking the medicine and swallowing it, I lay down as he said "Mom will be up in a minute. Don't feel so bad Deedy. That dish wasn't important. You lie down now and wait for Mom, she'll be up soon."

Then he did the strangest thing that again brought a torrent of unstoppable tears from my eyes. He bent over and kissed my forehead. Closing my eyes tightly to lock in the flood that was pouring out of them, I pressed myself into the bed and buried myself in the pillow. The shaking within me was completely out of control.

"Here darling now sit up and drink this." Mother sat down on the edge of my shaking bed and put her hand on my arm. I had trouble holding the cup of hot milk without spilling it. We sat there while I sipped a little at a time until finally I gained some control over my body. Mother's warmth began to penetrate the coldness I felt even though she wasn't holding me. She loved me. The whole idea was overpowering. She loves me, her daughter who is so guilty of lying, such an accomplished deceiver. Her daughter who was the next thing to being a whore.

As I finished the last sip of warm milk, my insides had finally emptied out. No more painful feelings. They had all come out. Now I could sleep in peace.

"Good night darling and have happy dreams." She left the room noiselessly. I was alone in the darkness of my emptiness. I'm so sorry Mama. 'I didn't mean to' echoed inside my mind. Somehow I slept through the night. The next week passed without a single mention of the Wedgewood platter. It was gone now, just a fragment of memory, Not real.

New Year's Eve arrived and again and this year would be different than all the New Year's Eve celebrations I remembered.

This was supposed to be a time to celebrate, but instead of being a ritual, New Year's Eve was a time for grown-ups to have fun and act with crazy abandon. Through the years, I witnessed many New Year's Eve parties that brought cultured, composed friends to my parent's home for the purpose of celebrating the passing of the old year. Mother had loved to host parties and took tremendous effort to plan and arrange every detail so that each hors d'oeuvre, each decoration, and each item used to bring in the New Year would bring great pleasure. She was very creative, and every party she hosted had her special touch of originality to it. She never served just cheese and crackers or chips and dips, but instead made canapés and hot hors d'oeuvres. The decorations that loudly claimed "this is New Year's Eve," adorned the table that was brimming with delicate morsels, and also filled the living room, den and guest bathroom. There was no way of escaping the fact that it was a special party in our house. The guest list had been carefully made up to match each guest to another who had something in common. The chairs throughout the area were grouped in such a way that if someone chose to sit, there would always be a seat next to them to be filled by some captivating individual ready for entertaining companionship.

*୬-୬-୬-୬-୬*

I remember in our old house sitting at the bottom of the stairs secretly spying on the parties, and no one ever knew I was watching. The stairs were in a hall off the dining room and had a door at the bottom that concealed my hiding place. I would adjust the door, so it looked like it was closed but was, in fact, opened just enough of a crack so I could see everything that went on without being observed. Those adults amazed me.

Some of them were the parents of my friends, and I had seen them in their homes where they behaved the way mothers and fathers do. They were grown-ups and acted like grown-ups. But at these parties, which Mother had so thoughtfully and creatively planned, something happened to the guests.

As I sat concealed behind the door in my secret place, I watched as changes took place in the behavior of these people who I thought were composed, sophisticated, mature adults. As the hours passed, they would begin to talk louder and laugh louder. Some of the women began loud flirting with other women's husbands, and husbands put their arms around other wives and snuggle up to their ears to whisper things that I couldn't hear. Other adults got louder and dance more as though they wanted everyone to notice them. When midnight arrived, the behavior of everyone was completely crazy. Shortly before twelve o'clock, Mother distributed party hats that were made out of brightly colored paper and reminded me of the ones I use to wear at birthday parties. She then gave each guest a cardboard whistle that had strips of paper dangling from the end of it. There were bowls full of confetti for everyone to throw up in the air and balloons waving above everyone's head. At the stroke of midnight, Mother turned off all the lights and then turned on a song called 'Auld Lang Sign.' Every year she played the same song and every year the lights went out. I don't know what went on after the lights were off, but the noise these adults managed to make was tremendous and sounded so happy. There were shouts of laughter, singing, and I'm sure I heard kissing. Corks on Champaign bottles burst up toward the ceiling, and glasses rang out as they were tapped together. Whistles blew and balloons popped. These adults had somehow stopped being adults and became just like kids. They threw off their respectable coverings of restraint and removed all the inhibitions they must have been storing over the past twelve months. I loved to listen to them. I loved the thought that they could be just as silly as my friends and I could be. The entire night gave me a wonderful feeling and made me think that being an adult might not be as boring as it usually appeared.

✼ ✼ ✼ ✼ ✼

This year was completely different. No party had been planned. Mother decided that she and Daddy were going to welcome in the New Year together without company. She had planned to prepare a midnight supper of lobster tails and salad with Dad's favorite cheese, Camembert, spread on small pieces of toast.

Freddy and I were going to go to a party at Chuck's house. As mother was setting out the candles and silverware for their occasion, Freddy arrived and I prepared to leave with him. Chuck's mother and father would not be there since they were going to celebrate at someone else's house. Of course, Mother didn't know I was going to an unsupervised teenage party. She would never allow such a thing. We arrived late and as we entered the door, noisy laughter bombarded us along with a strong smell of beer and cigarettes which hung like a thick cloud in the air. The rug had been rolled up and carried out to the porch, leaving a dusty dance floor that was filled with stocking feet dancing to the sound of Chubby Checkers.

"Do you want a beer Deedy?"

"No, I don't think so."

"Oh, come on."

"Well, maybe I'll try just one."

And so my first New Year's Eve party had begun. The night was not what I had expected. I didn't have the fun I'd seen my parents have. The beer was not very pleasant, and I couldn't imagine why so many people seemed to like it. The air was so thick with smoke from cigarettes that it was difficult to breathe and made my eyes water. Freddy and I joined in with everyone else and danced, talked, laughed, and stopped now and then to nibble on the chips and dips and crackers that were on the table. The floor was covered with crumbs and spilled beer, and the kids were loud, and a few were even drunk. The entire party was a disappointment. It felt like everyone had become wild just because it was New Year's Eve. As soon as I heard Chuck shout out, "It's twelve midnight," I said to Freddy "I want to leave. Will you take me home?"

That night, after taking off my New Year's Eve clothes and putting on my warm flannel nightgown, I climbed into bed and held my pillow as close as possible, hugging it the way I had hugged my doll years ago and cried until I saw the light begin to filter through my windows. Morning was here, and it was the New Year. I would be sixteen this year and officially old enough to drive. I would turn Sweet Sixteen.

I cried and cried and cried until eventually I fell into a deep dark hole that swirled around and around making me sick and dizzy. Holding on to the pillow as I went into the hole. I got out of bed and fumbled my way to my closet and took all the pills that were left. I swallowed six capsules hoping the pain would go away. Hoping to find some escape from my disappointment, from my longing to feel good and from my constantly nagging guilt. Swallowing them down with a glass of water as I stood in front of the mirror over the sink, I wondered what was going to happen to me. What was the point of my battle? Looking into the mirror, I saw my face staring at me with an expression of contempt. I didn't say anything. I just stared, rejecting the face in the mirror. I returned to my bed telling myself as I walked that everything was alright. Capsules loomed in front of me and fear surged through my mind like a hot compress, pushing me down. I was weightless as I floated down.

I shut my thoughts out of my head and said, "I know Freddy loves me, and that is enough to keep me going." As I lay my head down, the room began to spin and tilt sideways. It felt as though my bed was falling through the floor. Closing my eyes, the image of six hugely oversized pills pushed me down, down. I knew I had taken too much medicine this time. Too many pills at one time. They will find out. I left my body, and I left my room and floated far away to nothingness until I found peacefulness.

# Chapter Seventeen

## Sixteen Years Old

It had been two months since I'd seen Dr. Branscom and was "officially" considered "well" by everyone. Thank heavens being "well" didn't mean I had to stop my medicine. Since that awful night last New Year's Eve when I took so many pills, I forced myself to cut back to only three before going to bed. No one had ever found out what happened to me. Looking back on that morning, I realized that I almost lost all the control I'd been fighting to hold on to. If anyone had found out what happened, the pills would probably have been taken the away, and that terrified me. The memory of that terrible morning was still vivid. When Mother woke me up around noon on New Year's Day, I felt completely drained of life and so weak that I knew if I tried to get up, I would not be able to support my weight. Somehow, I convinced Mother that I must have the flu and should sleep all day. She left my room, and as I started to fall back into a deathlike sleep, the fleeting thought of danger passed through me. Too much medicine. Much too much.

It was dinner time before Mother woke me up again, but I felt as if I still hadn't slept. The image of oversized pills again flashed through my mind, and I knew I could never take so many again. Now I would have to fight the awful weakness and force myself up. Somehow I had to appear as though I was recovering from a short bout with the flu.

As I lay in bed, I pictured my muscles gathering strength, getting hard and strong. After enough tension built up and my muscles had gained some strength, I forced myself to rise from my bed. Sweat was trickling down my back and over my forehead. Thick nauseating liquid came up from my stomach and lodged in my throat as my head pounded from inside. Finally, I was able to get myself into the bathroom. After vomiting and vomiting and crying and vomiting, I rested my exhausted body against the tile floor. My body quivered as the spasms began to ease. The stench lodged in my nostrils like curdled milk. My stomach gave one last convulsive dry heave. There was nothing left. "My God, I had escaped. NEVER again. Never!"

Ever since that awful day, I had only taken three capsules at night which was no longer enough to make me float the way I used to. But since I had to protect myself, I decided I would have to live without that. I would try to get a good feeling in my mind by envisioning happy things.

Another recent memory about my secret pills flashed through my mind. Freddy had been on the stage getting ready to give one of his speeches and I was distraught over the fact that I knew he would be graduating very soon. We were driving to his apartment after school when somehow I forgot he was sitting next to me. I started to take some pills from my purse oblivious that he was watching. His voice shocked me when he asked, "What are you taking?"

How could I forget he was there? As I fumbled with the pills, almost dropping them, I answered, "Oh, it's just time for my medicine." I fought against my emotions and tried to calm down.

Freddy immediately said, "You don't need so many of those pills. They just make your eyes look glassy, and you sound like you don't know what's going on around you when you talk."

"Freddy, I have to take my medicine. Dr. Branscom has said I may have to take it the rest of my life so you'd better get used to it!" After pausing a moment, I added, "It helps me forget about that awful man." When I finished my last sentence, the expression on Freddy's face told me I had said the right thing. His face had softened as creases on his forehead pulled his eyebrows up making a deep furrow in his brow and he reached over and took my hand.

He parked the car by the nearest curb and turned off the motor. Changing the position of his body and turning in my direction, I was able to see the compassion and concern in his eyes. He pulled me close, encircling me with his arms in a protective vise-like hold. "You know I'll protect you from him. You don't ever have to think about it again." As he spoke, I could feel my body begin to relax.

I had said just the right thing. Several months before, when I had referred to "that man" and watched Freddy's reaction, I realized immediately that whenever I wanted him to understand whatever I had said or was feeling all I would have to do would be to mention the rape or the man. Freddy told me about his alcoholic father and how rough he had been with his mother before she divorced him ten years ago. He said that what had happened to me reminded him of the way his father had treated his mother, and he hated him for it. Any mention of my experience brought a flood of protective emotions from him. I had used my newly found verbal tool several times on Freddy but now he had become so overly protective that I felt he was smothering me with a demanding possessiveness. He began to question my every move and demanded to know what I did with my time when we weren't together. His questions had begun to sound like Mother's.

Chapter Eighteen

# His Senior Prom

His Senior Prom was coming soon and he had felt I would not be allowed to go with him. He was sure Mother would say no. I told him I had a feeling that because I would be sixteen next month and since we would be double dating with Chuck and Kristin, she would probably let me go, and I was right. For many years, I believed Senior Proms were the most wonderful experiences a girl could ever have, and now I was one of the lucky ones to attend one. Not very many girls in my grade were asked. Ever since I was a little girl, I knew there were three very important things that could happen to a young woman in her lifetime, and one was her first Prom. And now, I was going to experience this first event on Friday night with Freddy. The other two things would come later and would also be with Freddy; to marry and to give birth.

When the morning of the Prom day finally arrived, I woke up with a giddy, light-headed sensation and was sure if I tried to eat breakfast, nothing would stay down. It's too bad I even had to go to school. I jumped up from the bed and ran to the top of the stairs yelling down, "Mother, do I have to go to school today? Please let me stay home to get ready for tonight."

"No, Deedy. You'll have plenty of time when you get home." A heavy disappointment filled me. I knew all of the seniors, including Freddy, would not be at school today. I was sure the day would be awfully long and lonely, and the other students would ignore me. Without Freddy and his friends, what would I do during lunch? Maybe Kristin and I could eat together. "Deedy, hurry up, or you'll be late for school." Mother's voice reminded me of how late it had gotten, so I ran down the stairs, grabbed the glass of juice and gulped it down. Picking up my books from the table, I flew out the front door and headed for the bus stop while fumbling in my purse for my pills.

The school was ghost-like as I walked down the hall to my locker and wove my way through a group of tenth-grade boys. I carried my books in my left arm while holding my stomach in to make it flat and firm looking. My muscles were tense as I held my shoulders rigidly and my head high and directed my eyes straight in front of me, not so much as glancing in the direction of a single boy. I knew the outside of me was pretty. I had made sure of that this morning. I knew that my skin was deeply tanned and that my hair was a blond shade that gave me a healthy, sunny look, but somehow the inside of me didn't match. There was tightness in my throat, and the skin on my arms felt cold while a warm clamminess emanated from under my arms and down my back. As I looked straight down the hall, I felt the little beads of perspiration on my nose and upper lip. The walls of the hall lined with lockers seemed to be falling in toward the center of the floor while the stairs at the end were waving up and down. I could hear a faint buzzing sound from somewhere inside my head. As soon as I had safely passed the group of boys, I walked into the bathroom. Pushing the door closed, I leaned my back against the wall and took several deep breaths, then reached inside my purse to the hidden pocket where I kept the pills. I could feel sweat trickling down my scalp as I quickly put a pill in my mouth and swallowed the small lump.

I heard the bell ring, and knew I would be marked tardy for my first class, but didn't care. What difference did it make? Ever since last October when I was elected as a Student Body Representative for the tenth grade I had been able to come up with some excuse as to what business I had been taking care of. Thinking back to discovering the students in my grade actually voted me as a Student Body Representative had made no sense to me! How did that ever happen? It had to be a mistake! Ever since the election, I was sure my name must have gotten mixed up with a different name and I wasn't really supposed to be there. Someone else had been elected, and I was terrified that the mistake would be discovered. I would be utterly humiliated! Oh well, that was last October, and the school year was almost over now and no one ever found out the truth! Could I really have been elected? If so, was it because I'm Freddy's girlfriend? I couldn't think about it any longer, it was too confusing. Most of the kids in my grade never even talked to me let alone elect me. I was much more comfortable with the senior class students and felt like I belonged with them much more than those in the tenth grade. Everyone in the senior class liked me and thought I was important. Some of Freddy's friends even flirted with me, making him show jealousy. The boys in the tenth grade were so different and still didn't pay any attention when I was around them. It had been that way ever since I returned to school after that awful man took me away, and I suppose it will always be that way.

I got home after struggling through the day and made preparations for my special Prom night to finally arrived.

After carefully getting dressed, I looked into the full-length mirror and was thrilled with the way I looked. My skin was tanned to a beautiful color of copper brown and was smoother than ever. My long hair looked just the shade of blond I liked.

The beautiful Lanz dress that I had borrowed from Suzie to wear to the Prom was straight out of a fairy tale and fit me perfectly. It had tiny spaghetti straps attached to a form-fitting bodice with a full skirt that gathered softly at the waist. The fabric was delicate to the touch and of a blue shade so light it almost looked white. Mother and I had difficulty finding a pair of shoes to match the dress because of Freddy's height. He was only two inches taller than I was and he didn't like it when I wore high heels. Mother and I searched and searched all over for a pair of dressy, low-heeled shoes which would be the same light shade of blue as the dress. After going to five stores, we finally gave up and purchased a low-heeled pair of white satin shoes and took them to a shoe store to be dyed to match the dress.

When Mother paid to have the shoes dyed to match my dress, and we left the store, I felt a tremendous urge to hug her, but something stopped me and I couldn't reach out to her. Something strong held my arms back. It was as though my arms weighed hundreds of pounds and were too heavy to lift. After all, it was Mother who had made me tell all those lies. It was she who pried into my life and wouldn't leave me alone. Why should I even want to hug her? But when I thought about all the time she had just spent with me, choosing the right shoes, I became confused and full of anger toward her. All that came out of my mouth was "Thank you, Mother."

Even after she picked up the shoes from the store and proudly showed me how perfectly they matched the dress, my confused emotions still took over. After seeing how beautiful my entire outfit was all I could do was say, "Thank you, Mother. " Then I abruptly grabbed the packages from the table and ran upstairs to my bedroom. I never did hug her for all she had done for me.

Prom time finally arrived and I heard the doorbell ring downstairs. After carefully viewing my image in the full-length mirror, I flew down the steps to find Mother had already opened the door and invited

Freddy inside.

He slipped a beautiful corsage of white orchids on my wrist and Mother took several photos of us.

*Prom night with Freddy.*

The entire night was like a fairy tale. Freddy and I had danced in the dimly lit room, and I was Cinderella in the arms of my prince charming. Closing my eyes heightened my sense of his masculine strength. As he guided me effortlessly through the other dancing couples, a viral essence filled my nostrils reminding me of his lusty manhood, which was well hidden behind the pale blue formal evening clothes he had chosen to wear. The after-shave lotion that mingled with his natural scent only served to reinforce his maleness.

Our bodies were pressing so close that I could feel every ripple that passed through his well-muscled arms and chest. A firm tension came from his upper thighs and seemed to frame the enlarged bulge that protruded from his groin. Undefined images of a man and woman gently and romantically making love through a veiled cloudiness filled my eyes. Sensuous aromas, tingling sensations, and soft melodious sounds were pushing my emotions to such a passionate peak that I felt defenseless and on the verge of collapsing. The entire evening passed by in a dream-like haze. Freddy and I never attempted to satisfy our aroused conditions, but instead maintained a pitch of passionate desire that created an intoxicating excitement. We floated through the evening on invisible clouds until he brought me to my front door and gently pushed his lips against mine and whispered, "Good night, my beautiful love."

A day had passed since that wonderful night with Freddy at the Prom. I was lying on the air mattress floating in the swimming pool in my backyard trying to get my skin even darker so it would be the same as the rich coppery color I had seen in the Coppertone ads. My eyes had been closed as I was floating on the still surface of the cool chlorinated water under the soothing, almost hot rays of the sun. The warming sensation penetrated through my skin without interruption. There was not even the slightest wisp of a cloud in the vividly, pure, blue sky. A very slight breeze gently and continuously blew around keeping my skin comfortably cool despite the 85 degree temperature. When the warmth finally left I got myself out of the pool and went upstairs to dress.

"What's the matter Deedy?" Mother's prying question followed me up the stairs, and I yelled back, "Nothing. The sun left and I got cold."

As I went into the bathroom I felt relief at the memory my period had finally started on Monday morning before the Prom on Friday. The fear and tension of waiting for my periods to start had taken over too much of my time lately. Ever since the end of last December, my period had been so irregular that I never knew when it was supposed to start. It had seemed like I spent half of every month just waiting. The waiting became such a familiar part of every month that when it started I was filled with wonderful relief.

This would be my first day back to school since the Prom and I wanted to look good. The seniors would be at school for one more week as they prepared for their graduation ceremony. As I looked in my closet determined to pick the most flattering outfit I owned to wear, anger and frustration welled up inside me at the sight of how crowded all my clothes were. Only about four or five outfits were decent enough to wear, but Mother wouldn't let me throw away the rest because she had a strange idea that people should keep their old clothes.

"Styles keep changing Deedy and clothes that are not in style today will come back in style later." I shut my ears to her voice and continued to throw away my old outdated dresses. But when she saw them in the trash can, she would rescue them saying, "Keep this. It will come back in style Deedy. Mark my word. I've seen it happen too often."

I angrily pushed the ugly old clothes that she insisted I keep as far into the corner of my closet as possible, knocking some dresses to the floor. Then I neatly arranged the three skirts, four blouses and four dresses that looked good in an orderly fashion. They were each of a nice shade of blue ranging from the lightest to the darkest navy. Stepping back, I studied each item carefully, deciding on the light blue blouse and navy skirt. Most of my outfits were of different shades of blue. Freddy liked me in blue, so that is all I ever wear. Taking longer than usual to dress, I went to the full-length mirror in Mother's room to survey the results of my choice. As I slowly turned around carefully examining every possible angle, a sense of pride filled me for a fleeting moment.

Well, maybe I did have to work hard to achieve the look I wanted. So what if I had added a little lemon juice to the top and sides of my hair to help it become blonder when in the sun! No one knew that it wasn't natural. So what difference did it make if it wasn't natural! Maybe my thighs and legs were a little too thick, but when I wore the right skirt and shoes, no one else could see what was underneath. Taking Mother's hand mirror, I turned my back to the full length mirror, studying the back of my image that reflected in the glass in front of my eyes. Oh no! Again I checked to make sure I was right. The hem of the stupid skirt was hanging down and needed mending. I looked at the watch on my wrist as panic poured through my body.

Slamming the mirror to the floor, I ran out of Mother's room swinging the door against the wall. I tore the skirt off, running back to my closet to choose a different one. "Nothing matches!" Tearing my blouse off and throwing it against the wall, I angrily grabbed another blue blouse and the white skirt. Zippering it roughly, I ran back into Mother's room to again check myself, pulling my shoulders up so my back was straight giving me height. Freddy didn't like me to look tall, but I wasn't even sure I would see him at school today. I wanted to look tall. Tall and proud. Approving of my image in the full-length mirror, I reached down and picked up the hand mirror that was on the floor. The glass was cracked. "Stupid mirror!" Turning my back, I again examined my image from behind. When looking into the glass, there were two of me. Two faces that looked like each other. They were the same, except one stopped half way through my head and then the other one started, giving me two bodies; neither of which was complete. An overpowering weakness filled me, making me have to sit on the edge of Mother's bed. I sat there breathing deeply to regain my control and caught a glimpse of myself in the full-length mirror. There was only one Deedy. Only one! I placed the broken mirror on the table next to Mother's bed and went downstairs to wait for Mother to get the car out because she was going to drive me to school today.

The heat of summer warmed the air as the time arrived when Kristin and I would be in the audience and watch as Freddy and Chuck received their diplomas and then throw their caps in the air to celebrate

Kristin took my hand and led me into the auditorium where we would watch the seniors receive their graduation certificates. We were both somewhat excited and sad at the same time since this meant Freddy and Chuck would be leaving us behind. She pulled me toward the two empty seats near the front of the auditorium. When we sat down, I was acutely aware of the loneliness that engulfed me and wondered how someone could be sitting in the middle of a mass of people and yet be so totally alone. Now that Freddy was graduating from high school, I wasn't sure how I would survive. He was sitting on the stage with the other student body officers waiting to give his speech and looked so confident. I tried to ignore the coldness emanating from the unyielding, hard surface of the folding chair I was sitting on.

My mind drifted back in time as I crawled deep into my memories of the past few months. During the past year, ever since I entered high school, I felt like I belonged as long as Freddy and his friends were around. They had given me a special spot among all the hundreds of other students at the school. Freddy was very outgoing and made everyone laugh with the clownish humor he displayed. We'd be walking down the hall, talking when suddenly he would appear to trip dropping a book and acting so silly that laughter rang out all around him. He had earned the title of "class clown." His eyes constantly danced and a slight smile appeared to be playing at his mouth while he would stop and talk to each and every student he knew. Freddy was a fairly good student. He even spent time memorizing the dictionary so he could sound educated and smart. Freddy had lots of ambition and wanted to go to college and make lots of money. He had worked hard at getting good grades in high school.

I didn't care about my grades and never worried about them. I didn't have to because, as I learned long ago, the teachers passed me no matter what I did. Ever since I was thirteen and that awful man took me away, I had not been able to work for a single grade because of my lost memory. All the teachers gave me at least a C grade, whether or not I earned it. With the help of my medicine and with Freddy as my boyfriend, the school year had gone by terribly fast and now it was all over. I would be alone when I returned to school. The past year was gone and was only a fragment of time that had passed by me. That time had been full of wonderful events that only punctuated my current overwhelming sense of loneliness. School would be so different next year when he was gone.

Suddenly, I was shocked back to the present when Kristin grabbed my hand pressing it firmly into hers, with tears forming in her eyes. The ceremony was finished, and our boyfriends were standing on the stage holding their diplomas and shaking the hands of well-meaning teachers who were congratulating them. Everyone around us was getting up to join the graduates. Kristin and I pushed through the people who were standing in various small groups that were sprinkled among the many bodies milling around. We pushed through the crowds and finally reached Freddy and Chuck. I felt far outside of everything in the room and everyone around me. As I looked at the animated faces of the graduating seniors, a tremendous stab of jealousy pierced me. They were going on to a more exciting life and did not ever have to return to high school. After what seemed like an eternity of voices saying "Congratulations," and asking, "What are you going to do now?" It seemed like a million people were aimlessly walking around in slow motion.

The best wishes finally ended and we left to get some pizza before going on to several graduation parties. The rest of the evening flew by in a sped-up blurred vision of people dancing, kissing, drinking beer and laughing at invisible humor. I felt like I was outside of everything. Freddy was irritated at me when I reminded him that Mother expected me home by midnight. As we drove home I watched the blue angora dice I had knitted for him as a graduation gift bob up and down, up and down, as they hung on his rear view mirror. I felt unable to talk or to share in the exuberance Freddy displayed.

My head throbbed with a pulsing hotness as I struggled to breathe through the thickness in my throat. I could hear heavy breathing inside my head. It vibrated against the insides of my ears. School would be so different next year with Freddy and his friends gone. I would be alone when I returned to school after summer. The past year was gone and was only a fragment of time that had passed by me. That time had been full of wonderful events that only punctuated my current overwhelming sense of loneliness.

⚜⚜⚜⚜⚜

Suddenly I heard a voice inside my brain say, "It's all over. I told you it wouldn't last." I shut my lids tightly against my aching eyes to force the voice away. That voice had been gone so long. I thought it was dead. "I told you no one would ever want you. You're a bad girl! You're scarred and ugly." I pulled the sweater that was draped over my shoulders up and around my head pressing its softness against my ears to block out the taunting voice.

⚜⚜⚜⚜⚜

"What are you doing Deedy?" Pierced through in a deep voice that sounded like Freddy's. The images in my mind were swirling around making me helplessly fall into a dark pit of nothingness when suddenly someone grabbed my hands and forcefully held on. I looked up to see Freddy's eyes staring in disbelief at me while his mouth made motions of speech without any sounds coming from it. I could see he was shaking me but could not feel it.

"What do you want?" I heard my voice asking.

"What's the matter with you? What are you doing?" He asked in a frantic tone of voice.

"I just have an awful headache, Freddy, I'll be alright." His arms moved tightly around as I avoided looking at him. There was no feeling of warmth coming from his hug. My body was so cold, and I felt so far away from him that it was as though he wasn't even touching me at all.

That night, when we got to my house, he said, "I'll call you first thing in the morning and hope you feel better. You look awful."

I took an extra pill before going to bed, but it didn't keep the voice from reaching me through most of the night. In a dream, I saw a girl who was dressed in a silly virginal white dress dancing around in front of me while I tried to shield myself from her. A voice repeated over and over again, "You are very ugly and very bad. He doesn't want you. He will leave you very soon."

During the summer months, Freddy was working every day and I spent my time going to the beach with my girlfriends. I felt lonely without Freddy and spent hours at the beach feeling angry because he spent so little time with me. We did go to a couple of movies and we did make love several times, but not nearly as much as we had during the school year.

Many times he asked me what I did during the days while he worked. Over and over again I answered him saying, "You know what I do. I go to the beach and meet my friends or sometimes they come to my house and we swim in the pool. I've told you the same thing every time you ask. Don't keep asking me. Why do you have to work every single day? If you would come to the beach with me you could see what I do, and you wouldn't have to ask. You almost sound like you don't trust me."

One evening late in August nearing the end of summer vacation, we were sitting in Freddy's car in front of his apartment building watching the sunset when he said, "I want to trust you Deedy. Except when I'm working all day and know that you're at the beach, I picture you with other boys. We used to be so close, but since summer started, you hardly talk anymore. You seem so far away, it's like you don't care about me anymore. Is there someone else? What's wrong? Tell me what is going on with us?"

I felt suffocated by his words. My lungs had collapsed and would hold no more air. The pressure on my chest would not let me breathe and I whispered the words, "When you're working all day every day, I'm lonely. What happened to the way you used to trust me? It sounds like you don't have any trust in me now and only complain about me?"

"No, I trust you Deedy. It's just that I love you so much and don't want to lose you," he responded.

"Then leave me alone. Just stop prying into everything I do as if you don't trust me. Stop asking me so many questions."

My head involuntarily turned toward his direction and saw his eyes staring with the most vulnerable and saddest look ever. He'd turned everything around. It's all because he's been working. How can we be close when he leaves me alone all the time? I was sure he didn't trust me. Just like Mother. Too many people thought they owned me. I didn't belong to him, I belong to myself! When I looked into those wonderful blue eyes of his and saw only the hurt and rejection that came from them, I wanted to reach out to him and to hold him. To tell him he was confused. I wasn't rejecting him. But I couldn't reach out. Shame and guilt filled me to my deepest depth. It had been there for so terribly long that I couldn't reveal its secret.

My control was beginning to drain away so I dug my fingernails deeply into the palms of my hands so I would feel pain. When I felt myself physically hurting, I could hold on to control. I pressed my teeth together until it felt as though they were being pushed back into their roots. I released the tension and felt pain in the joints of my jaws that traveled up around to the front of my head. I concentrated on curling my toes inside my shoes until a sharp cramp paralyzed the arch of my foot. As long as I concentrated on feeling the pain, I didn't have to think. I had control.

As I left him that day and looked at his face through the open window before turning to go into my house, I felt an overpowering need to run. To run from all the hard, sharp edges that projected from reality.

# Chapter Nineteen

## Run

I needed to run someplace, anyplace away from everything. I had to hide my shame and the overpowering guilt inside me. I needed to hide. I couldn't reveal the fact that I was flawed to the core with weakness, with lies, with cheating, with the knowledge that I had been awful for so long. I opened the front door to find everyone gone and inside the emptiness rose up at me with an aggressive attempt to bury me.

I was submerged under enemy attack and fled as fast as I could up the stairs to find the welcoming warmth of my bedroom. As I stepped into my pink refuge, a voice pierced the deafening silence with a whisper of "ugly ugly ugly." "Rotten to the core. Bad, bad, bad. Bad tramp. Bad." The bathroom. I'll be safe there. I can get away. Reaching into the medicine cabinet over the sink, I found the lethal blade to my brother's razor and safely slipped it into the pocket of my shorts. I'll kill the voice if it doesn't stop. I knew I couldn't stand the voice any longer. Lies. Lies.

As the walls of my attacker closed in on me with a speed that would surely bury me within seconds, I ran and fell, ran and fell, ran and fell down the endless staircase throwing the front door open violently against the wall behind it, fighting to leave the enemy far behind. The evening air hit my face, entering my nostrils and filling my mouth with a coldness that made me aware of feeling; the feeling of suffocation. Feeling the throbbing of my enemy. Feeling the machine inside take control and carry me away.

I needed to escape. I ran as fast as possible down the sidewalk that led me through the darkness of the night air without a guiding light to show the path. Thousands of eyes were staring accusingly; knowingly peering into the deepest most secret parts of my being. Voices filled my head so full it would soon burst from the pressure; "You should have fought." "You are ugly." "I'm going to make you even uglier!" "Scars!" "I'm going to kill you!" I swam through the voices and ran from the faces only to get caught up in a whirlpool that sucked me down. The forces of the pool were fueled by a dark loneliness. Unbearable loneliness right in the middle of a thousand faces and voices. I was so very alone and exposed. The smallest protective shred of dignity had left me. My soul was alone without any covering. I was left vulnerable to the cutting edges of reality which constantly prodded, pounded, and poked at each flaw, at each thread of weakness, making me see no beauty, feeling no pride; leaving me hopelessly isolated, wallowing in the solitude of shameful guilt.

I reached far into my jumbled thoughts, clambered into my mind to hunt for the friendly environment that I knew was in there. Fantasy land. Cinderella! Snow White! Alice in Wonderland! They had all overcome their problems. I would overcome mine. Conquer! But exhaustion rendered me helpless to fight anymore as I ran on and on. Why would anyone even want to fight their way into the raging pain of reality? Escape, escape from the battle. I forced open the heavy lids that shielded my eyes from life to find my body leaning against the rough, splintery timbers of framing in an unfinished apartment building that was far from comfort. The damp earth beneath my legs was littered with indications that some other humans had been there.

Cigarette butts. Wrappers. Nails. Smells. Dirt. My soul was somewhere embedded within the shell I saw as I looked down at me. Taking out the weapon that I had concealed in the pocket of my virginal white shorts, the sharpness of the edge slipped, bringing forth a dark flowing liquid which came from the tip of my index finger. There was life somewhere within, it was trying to escape from the shell. I was empty as I watched the darkness of the liquid spread over to the finger that lay next to the wounded one to share in the false impression of pain. There was no pain. No feeling. The shell covered nothing. Grasping the thin blade between my thumb and index finger of my darkened hand, I lay down to rest before finding my escape. Now I lay me down to rest. Pray the Lord will give me peace. Closing my eyelids I saw on their inside surface the warm cloud covered path to a beautiful flower garden where my prince was sitting on the edge of a large smooth rock looking at me. My prince's eyes held all the varying shades of the rainbow within them and with a light of love. I was wearing a soft white dress with a long lace train that gently flowed from my waist. The fabric felt good against my skin and was made of threads as fine as the silk of a spider's web. A bouquet of newborn daisies, lilies of the valley, and white roses were protectively held in the grasp of my relaxed hand. The silkiness of the rich colored green grass felt refreshingly comfortable under my bare feet. My eyes were partially hidden behind the symbolic veil that was gently fastened under the halo of white roses resting on my beautiful golden hair.

As I came closer to my prince, the distance grew. I ran and ran to his outstretched arms, but could not get any closer. I ran and ran feeling only the grass beneath me. Then gradually the wonderfully perfumed aroma coming from the garden turned sour. The garden flowers wilted and lay on the course brown grass-covered earth. Suddenly my handsome prince became a grossly oversized, greasy, dark haired, oily mustached man with menacing eyes that pierced through me. "If I should die before I wake. Pray to God. Take my soul."

It was over. Opening my eyelids again, feeling nothing, I sat up and licked the dark, salty dried liquid from my fingers. Taking the sharp edge of the blade, I began pressing it firmly against the fatty part of the inside of my hand right above the wrist. After seeing dark liquid trickle out of the fresh cut, the blade moved to another spot and again sliced through the skin. Soon there were half a dozen places where the skin had parted to reveal pools of blood. Holding my arm above my head, I watched as it ran down in several thin streams and dripped from my elbow to the ground below. I was fascinated by the total lack of pain, or for that matter, any feeling at all. Laying my other arm on the light blue blouse which covered my stomach, I tried to examine the thick vein that I knew ran the length of my wrist, only to disappear beneath the thickness of the skin further up my arm. The moonlight that filtered through the unfinished building was too dim for me to see the vein. I closed my eyes and lightly pressed the sensitive tip of my thumb over the place where I knew the vein ran. It was still there. I could feel the slight rise where it protruded. Taking the weapon in my right hand, I started to move its sharp edge back forth over the skin covered vein until I felt it give as the soft flesh parted, pouring forth a stream of dark, warm liquid that flowed out over my wrist, covering my hand and spilling onto my blouse and shorts. I was startled by the intensity of the throbbing pain. Looking at life pour out of the wound, panic grasped my throat making me choke with a sickening taste of revulsion that welled up from my stomach. Muscles convulsed sending sour vomit out. Unstoppable tears released themselves from imprisonment, as the death tool dropped to the ground, and a loud cry echoed, "Oh my God. Look what I have done?"

Not to die. I did not mean to die. "Oh God, don't let me die. Help me." Grabbing the wounded wrist and pressing my hand tightly over the cut, I forced it to close against impending death. I can't die. Help me. Please send help. "God in heaven, if you're there, help me. Please help me." For ever and ever, I sat paralyzed with the deep need to live. Holding my wrist, I locked in what life was left, pleading for help.

Eternities passed when I saw the shadow of a human looming above me and heard a deep voice say, "Here she is." "Get over here quickly." Through a haze of exhaustion, my body submitted to the hands that were moving it, carrying it away. My eyes closed, refusing to acknowledge either the voices or the faces that surrounded me.

# Chapter Twenty

## Shocked Into Nothingness

I opened my eyes and was confronted with grayness that felt vaguely familiar. A smell was in the air that made me think I'd been there before. As faint images of nurses filled my mind, I felt a heavy unwelcome sense of dread. Ugly memories flooded into my mind. What had I expected? The last time he had taken me away, I ended up here too. The room was quiet, only the sound of my breathing could be heard. As I looked through the familiar bars fastened to the sides of the bed, I was reminded of how awful this place was. There was no surprise when I discovered I could not move my body. I remembered being tied with the same ties too tightly and held to this mattress before and did not feel surprised. My back was stiff as memories filled my thoughts. I remembered past times when I had been held in the same position for hours. I wanted to move. There was no way the restraints holding me down would give so much as an inch. I wiggled my fingers and felt the insides of the mittens that covered my hands and reminded me that they were attached to the sleeves of the course gown that was on me. I had been here before. How long ago was that? A lifetime ago? Or maybe I'd always been here. Maybe the hazy memory of having been home was a dream. I could not remember. The only thing I was sure of was that somehow he had taken me away again. I could remember seeing his face. That was the last thing I remembered. I don't know where I was when he came, but I knew it was him again. I tried to move and found I could turn my head and even raise it slightly, but only slightly. Then the thing that was tied across my shoulders stopped further movement. The feeling was all too familiar. I knew what it meant, and I didn't want it again.

As I looked around at the dull gray painted walls, the colorlessness of the room, the drab ceiling and whiteness of the bed I was on, I felt dread in the pit of my stomach. The dread spread throughout my body as a nauseating fluid and lodged in my throat like a lump. As I stared at my surroundings, a sense of hopelessness penetrated the dread. The longer my body lay imprisoned the more my thoughts became overpowered by the knowledge that life had ceased to exist within me. I had become an empty vessel. Both my body and my mind had lost feeling. Everything was meaningless. He stole my life and bled me dry until only a vacuum remained. I was an empty shell. A hollow body. There was no cold, no heat, no pain, no pleasure. Total emptiness. Complete nothingness. The ghost of me lay there with closed eyes, seeing nothing, wanting nothing, no longer hoping or caring.

"She's been sleeping long enough. Let's see if we can wake her up?" The voice penetrated my vacuum but had no meaning.

My eyes opened to see a nurse's face that belonged to someone from my past. This face was the face of someone I had not liked. Someone who was icy cold. "Well, well. Look who's awake! And how do we feel Deedy?" My head automatically turned away from the staring face. "Well, aren't we talking today?"

My unfeeling mind pulled out a memory buried deeply in the invisible file inside my brain. She was the patronizing 'we' nurse. The one who never said 'I' or 'you.' Only 'we.' I remembered not liking her. Whenever she had entered a room, the air became cold with her iciness. She thought she was better than any of the patients. She was heartless.

"Aren't we going to cooperate, Deedy?" I stared at the gray paint on the wall next to my bed. "It won't do you any good to ignore, us. You know that. You've been here before and you know we have ways of helping you cooperate with us."

My head involuntarily turned back toward her voice. The face looked as though it was made out of cement; all white and chalky, as her mouth moved in a distorted way. There was no memory of a name. Another face was slightly behind the nameless one and was also staring down at me. It was a nicer face, warm with dark eyes that were set in dark skin and topped with a fresh, crisp white nurse's cap. This face belonged to someone with the name Betty. I had liked her. She called me Deedy and referred to herself as 'I' and said 'you,' never using 'we.'

"How long have I been here?"

The 'we' nurse answered, "Now 'we' don't have to worry about that. I'm glad 'we' decided to cooperate."

"I didn't ask you. Why don't you crawl back under your rock?"

"My, my, aren't 'we' feisty today!"

"Betty, can't I talk to you without her butting in?"

"Alice maybe it would be better if you let Deedy and me talk awhile. You go see what Judy was wanting. I'll call you if I need anything."

The 'we' nurse abruptly turned around and marched out of the room.

"How do you feel Deedy?"

"Fine, I guess. How did I get here? Did they catch him?" My questions came out in an emotionless monotone.

"You've been here for three days now. They found you in a building that was under construction. And, there was no one there with you."

"You mean he wasn't there? He must have left."

"You'll be talking to Dr. Branscom later today; you can ask her about that. Now I'd like to get you up. You've been laying here long enough."

As she was untying the restraints holding me securely to the bed, the memory of a dark empty place passed through my mind as if in slow motion. It had been cold and dirty. I could see blood dripping from somewhere and remembered feeling afraid I was dying. There had been a blue blouse and white shorts so covered with blood that the original color of white was hidden. No feelings. Void of emotions.

"He must have hurt me again," I said in an emotionless voice.

"You discuss that with Dr. Branscom Deedy." When Betty finished untying me, I moved to see how badly he had hurt me. My body was not sore. Except for my wrists. They were stiff, and my hands throbbed with a dull painless ache. I held them up and saw that they were encased in white bandages, and thought that's not so bad.

"What did he do to me?"

"Let's not talk about that Deedy. Here lean on me and try to get up. You might be a little wobbly at first. Here, hold on to my arm and lean on me."

I rested my hand on her arm not holding very tightly because I was sure I didn't need her support. I didn't feel weak or injured. As a matter of fact, I didn't feel anything at all, except numbness.

"I'm O. K. I don't need any help." As the last word passed through my lips, the room began to tilt to the left making me grab her arm tighter so I wouldn't fall over.

"Here hold on for a minute. You'll be alright. Just wait for a minute or so until you regain your balance."

I closed my eyes and held on to her arm, waiting for the room to stop tilting. After a short time, I reopened them to find the room was back where it belonged. She was smiling at me, and my mouth smiled back saying, "That was strange."

"Yes, Deedy. You've had two shock treatments and some medicine that is probably making you feel weak. Let's go for a short walk around the room until you feel a little stronger." I moved my left foot in front of my right one, sliding it across the cold linoleum floor being careful not to lift it. I slid the right one up to join the left one and then repeated the same procedure over again. I was aware of the weakness of my body and of how much effort it took to move my legs forward. I had an awareness that the floor was cold and that I was moving, but there were no feelings within my body. I was a machine whose go button had been pushed. My hands held onto Betty's arm as she guided me forward very slowly. After we had progressed to the middle of the room, we turned around and headed back toward the bed. By the time we reached it, my legs were Jell-O.

I sat down on the edge of the bed staring at my bandaged wrists and asked, "Did he do something to my legs?"

"Don't worry Deedy. Your strength will return very quickly. You've been laying down a long time, and your legs are weak."

I tried to fill in the blank memory of the past few days, but only fragments of images appeared. There was nothing revealed about what I'd been doing. Nothing to hold on too. There had been nurse-faces floating around me. I remember emptiness and a sense of danger. There were dark red pools of blood and the aroma of death, but that was all. "Why can't I remember anything?"

"The shock treatments have temporarily caused a loss of memory. It will come back." Shock treatments. The words were vaguely familiar and brought a sense of fear to me. Was that what had sucked all feeling from me leaving only a shell covered vacuum?

"What's that? Shock treatments?"

"You had them before Deedy. When you were here before. They help to clear your mind of confusion."

"Are you sure? Why can't I remember anything?"

"That will go away. How do you feel now? Let's try to walk again." We went through the same process, walking to the middle of the room and back to the edge of the bed. This time, it was a little easier. As we waited for a short time, I examined the bandages covering my wrists and wondered what was under them. Again Betty guided me away from the bed for another walk. This time, we went all the way to the other side of the room before returning to the bed.

"Do you think you are strong enough to take a nice warm bath Deedy?"

"Yea, I suppose so." As I sat on the edge of the bed, she went over to the closet and pulled out a bathrobe that was hanging on a knob inside the door. Next, she bent over to retrieve a pair of paper slippers that were on the floor and brought the items over to me. I held her arm as we went out the door and down the long gray corridor and into the big cold room that was lined with open showers. It was all so familiar to me that I wondered if I had ever really been away from here. She took me to a small room connected to a big shower room that had one bathtub in it. The room was so small that the bathtub filled it leaving only enough floor space for a small wood stool in the corner. There were no towel racks or hooks on the walls; just plain walls painted that same drab gray color. Betty turned the faucet on full, and the empty tub quickly filled with steamy clear water.

"You get in now Deedy, and I'll just sit here on the stool while you take a nice warm bath. It will feel good to you."

When I looked down at the bandages on my wrists, she said, "Don't you worry about those. I'll put fresh bandages on after your bath. I took off the robe and gown as Betty sat down to wait. She didn't seem to be watching me. As I stepped into the tub I again I glanced over to her, but she still wasn't looking at me as I lowered myself down submerging myself deeply under the water. I was aware of a warmth coming from the water, but it didn't penetrate into the numb void under my skin. After I was clean and dry, she re-bandaged my wrists as I watched. There were many dark lines cut into the skin, some of which had threads holding them closed. I couldn't remember how I got hurt and looked up to Betty for some answer.

"They're healing fine Deedy," she said as she took my arm and said, "Come on follow me. We're going to get something to eat."

I followed her into a small kitchen located just off a small office at the end of the hall and watched as Betty opened a refrigerator door and took out a dish of red jello and a small carton of milk. "You sit down over there Deedy." She said pointing to a table and chair that were in the corner of the room against the wall. "This will taste good and help bring your strength back. "Here. You sit down."

I slowly ate the jello tasting nothing. I wondered what had happened to me. I remembered Freddy, and that it was summer. I remembered going to the Prom and seeing the ocean waves sparkle in the moonlight. I knew Freddy had graduated from high school. But I wasn't sure whether it was the beginning of summer or the end. What had happened to me?

"Where is my Mother?"

"She's been to visit you twice, but you had just had shock treatments and were sleeping. She'll be back tomorrow."

After finishing the jello, I mechanically followed Betty through the rest of the day. That night after she turned out the light in the room, I lay on the coarse white sheets that felt like canvas and watched as fragments of the past slid through my memory. Bits and pieces of imagery. Nothing concrete. Nothing to hold on to or to reveal what had happened. There were slowly moving scenes with Freddy and me sitting in a car. Of us dancing. Faces appeared, Mother's and Daddy's. My brother's face was hazy. He was in college or high school. What month was it? I couldn't grab on to anything, not even what grade I was in, the tenth or the ninth, or maybe even the eleventh? The ocean sparkled with dancing jewels that blinded me. His face appeared, and he was hurting me again. It didn't hurt, it only bled. Dark red blood that was full of life and ran in tiny droplets into a huge black pool. Life had escaped from my shell and was drowning in the pool. I was strangely disconnected from everything, darting in and out of images. Feeling nothing. Someone was coming into my room, and I turned to see who had intruded into my world.

"Here drink this." It was the 'we' nurse, and she was holding a little cup full of water and another smaller cup half full of dark pink liquid.

"What is that?"

"It will help you sleep."

"No thank you."

"Take it Deedy. The doctor has prescribed it for you."

"No!"

"Either you take it or we'll have to give it to you in a shot. Now, which do you want?"

I turned my back to her and looked at the gray paint on the wall. The paint looked as though it had been applied with a brush, and the direction of each stroke was clearly visible and went in all different directions. The paint must have been thick because the ridges and valleys that the hairs in the brush had made were still there. They had not flowed together before the paint had dried. There were some light yellow spots where the thickest paint ridges had chipped off. One. Two. Three. Four chips. Five. Six. I was aware of the needle as it sharply jabbed the side of my hip to send the unwanted pink liquid into me. Five. Six. Seven. Eight. The paint strokes became rivers, and I floated into them. Floated into nothingness.

The next day, Betty was by the side of my bed when I woke up.

"It's time to get up now Deedy. Your mother will be here this afternoon, so I want you to shower and fix your hair." I followed her through the morning, showering, dressing, eating, sitting and waiting.

"Come, let's wait in the day room for your mother. She'll be here soon." We waited.

I had sensed Mother's presence before she entered the room. She had always had a uniqueness about her that made her different from everyone else in my world. Something about her smell or sound. I sat and waited. Her arms enclosed me tightly and held me firmly for a very long time. No words. I sensed that she loved me. I was aware of the warmth that emanated from her body. She held me more. And some more. I sat there letting her hold me. I sat and she hugged. After she had held me as long as she wanted she stepped back and looked.

"Well Deedy, how do you feel? We've been so worried about you."

"I'm fine."

"I've brought some paper and pencils. I thought maybe you might like to draw some pictures. I also brought some magazines for you to read and some ribbons for your hair."

"Okay."

"Darling, we love you so very much and want you to get well quickly." Her arms were around me again as I sat listening to her words.

"Why am I here? Did he hurt me again?"

"Who Deedy? Did who hurt you?"

"That awful man. Did he come and take me away again?"

"No. Don't you remember what happened?"

"No. I just remember seeing him again."

"He wasn't there Deedy."

"I thought I was going to die."

"Darling, you'll be fine."

"Tell me what happened."

"Dr. Branscom will be talking to you later this afternoon. She'll be able to help you with your questions."

I couldn't understand why she wasn't answering me and asked, "Can't you answer me? Don't you know what happened?"

"I want you to discuss this with Dr. Branscom. She will help you understand what happened."

"Why? Is it so terrible that you can't tell me? Did he rape me again? Did he do it again?"

"Deedy please wait until you talk to Dr. Branscom. It would be better to talk to her about everything."

My mind filled with images of people, many people all sitting around me, next to me. Crowds of bodies and faces surrounding me and yet I was alone, totally alone with no one to talk to. Mother and I were sitting together next to each other, but I still felt alone. The distance between us was so great that she might just as well have been halfway around the world. When she left, I saw her body walk out of the room but was unaware of feeling anything. No sadness. No despair. No warmth. Nothing.

This morning after breakfast Betty told me I would be seeing Dr. Branscom today. When the time arrived a nameless nurse guided me to the doctor's office so I could get the answers I kept asking. I was led to the small white cottage far away from the main building that we had just left. We had followed the path through the neatly trimmed grass to get here. I remembered that elves maintained the lawn at night after everyone was in bed. When we walked up the steps to the cottage door, I was aware of a familiar odor entering my nostrils, but could not identify it or even really smell it. Maybe it was coming from the many green plants that filled the room or maybe from the old magazines laying on the table or the half-filled ashtray.

I sat and waited. The soft chair my body was sitting on was also familiar. I sat and waited, and pictured the small women with dark hair I knew would be coming out of the closed door. She always wore her hair pulled tightly back from her face to form a small stiff bun at the back of her neck. I could imagine her white skin that was almost transparent, but could not see any features on the face. It was blank. I sat and waited. The door opened just as I knew it would, and the small women with the dark hair came out. Her face was complete now, and I recognized it as belonging to Dr. Branscom. I felt her hand as it took hold of my arm and guided my body through the door and over to a chair that she told me to sit on.

"I forgot what you looked like," was my first comment.

"That's understandable Deedy. You've had two shock treatments in three days, and it will take a little time before your memory returns."

"Why can I remember some things and not others"?

"We don't know why that happens, but we do know that it is only temporary. You will soon remember everything."

"Why am I here?"

"Do you remember anything Deedy?"

"No. Just his face."

"Whose face?"

"That awful man's. The one who raped me."

"Do you think he was with you?"

"Yes. He was with me. He took me away. He tried to kill me this time."

"Deedy, tell me everything you think happened."

"He tried to cut me up and kill me so I wouldn't tell anyone. I don't remember if he raped me again, but I suppose he did."

"Deedy, he was not with you. He did not take you away."

"Yes he did! I remember seeing his face."

"No Deedy, he was not with you. Do you remember the last time you were here at Westerly when I told you that the mind can play strange tricks on people?"

"Sort of." I lied.

"Your mind has done that to you again Deedy. It is playing tricks on you and hiding some things from you. Now, again we must try to unravel the confusion and discover what the truth is."

Truth. The word brought a strange sensation to the pit of my stomach.

"What are shock treatments?"

"You don't remember that either? Well, they are treatments that help clear some of the confusion from your mind so we can talk and try to find out what you have been thinking."

"I can't remember anything. Everything starts and then stops. I start to remember something and then it just sort of fades away so I can't hold on to it. I don't like it. I want to remember."

"You will. Now let's see what you do remember."

We talked. She talked. I had nothing to tell her. There was nothing. The rest of the session did not reveal anything to me about what had happened, and Dr. Branscom did not tell me.

"Why won't you tell me why I'm here?"

"When your mind is ready to know, you will remember. It is best for you to remember at the proper time."

The nameless nurse led me back to the main building. She had to use a key to open the front door because it was always locked. After we had walked through it there was another door with a glass window full of wire mesh, and she pushed a button next to it that rang a bell inside so another nurse would come to open the second door.

# Chapter Twenty One

## Endless Vacant Time

We were inside now and the beginning of an endless vacant time had started. They gave me medicine. I ate and slept. They tied me to the bed and put me to sleep. I bathed and ate. They gave me shock treatments and my memory got worse. They walked me and fed me. They locked me into a bathtub full of ice water. They gave me pink liquid and I floated away. I ate. I slept. I stood under the shower water. I lay in bed. The ridges and valleys of gray paint were my road map to nowhere. I floated down the gray rivers and around the yellow chips. I woke up to nothing. I didn't know if I was at home or floating away. I ate and watched the gray colors on the television set. I slept. I swallowed pills and drank pink liquid. Mother looked at me and tears fell from her eyes. She hugged me. I felt nothing. I sat there. I ate and slept. I had shock treatments. I could not walk. I crawled. I was tired. Always tired. All I ever wanted to do was sleep. Sleep. Oblivion. Meaningless sleep. I woke up and was tired and wanted to go back to sleep. They made me walk and wouldn't let me crawl.

Time didn't move. There was no time. It had ceased to exist. One day someone told me it was the end of September. I asked someone else what year it was. I heard the number 1957. I had counted four hundred and thirteen little yellow chips in the gray river, not 1957. Then a voice said it was Halloween. Wasn't that the time when funny people dressed up even funnier? I used to be a lavender angel with wings. Mother pinned them on the back of my lavender dress. I was a lavender angel. I sat in the day room, and all the other ladies sat there too. Some of them talked, and some of them didn't. Dr. Branscom talked to me. My voice talked to her. She said nothing. My voice replied. Tears spilled out of Mother's eyes and ran down her face. Daddy's eyes were red-rimmed and full of tears too.

I wondered what was so sad. I didn't ask because I did not care. I had no cares. No feelings. I was mechanical and emotionless, encased in a shell that floated everywhere. Someone again said it was Halloween. I saw a pumpkin sitting on the table. Then I went to bed and drank the pink liquid and floated down my gray river.

I sat in the day room and saw the pumpkin. It had a face carved on the front, with a smile and two eyes and a nose. Something about it held my attention for the longest time. I couldn't take my eyes off of it. I looked and looked. As I watched the eyes and mouth it began to take a different shape. The nose and eyes came alive and turned into his awful face. His eyes pierced into my head, and he smelled greasy and dirty. My head was in a bubble and I could hear screaming all around, but the screams couldn't penetrate my bubble. Only his eyes pierced through my protective shield. Someone was screaming. I felt my arms being pushed into something and then being pulled behind my back so I couldn't move them. Someone was carrying me, but I couldn't feel it because the bubble protected me. The screaming was still trying to stab my bubble. Then the people who were carrying me put me down on a soft white pillow. I looked around and could hear screaming, but no one else was in the room. I was laying on a white pillow, inside of it. The screaming was beginning to hurt my ears, and my throat began to feel raw, so I pressed my ears against the pillow to lock out the noise. I could push myself against the pillow and only feel the softness. It felt good, so I pushed myself harder and faster until I was throwing my body at the softness over and over again. My throat was so raw it hurt. I tried to move my arms, but they were tied too tightly behind my back. I was hugging myself. I hugged tighter and tighter, and it felt good to be hugged. I rolled on the floor hugging myself when tears began to flow from my eyes in such a tremendous torrent that my body stopped trying to push them out. I threw myself over and over against the pillowed floor and against the pillowed walls repeatedly. I closed my eyes and could see the razor blade as it sliced through the skin on my wrists. I knew it had been me. I did it to myself. I did it. ME. I didn't want to die. I wanted help. Please, someone, help me. I saw my life flow out of the wound and cried for help. Please, someone, help me. If only someone would help me. I slammed against the wall again and again and again. I was as violent as I could be, and it felt good. I slammed myself continually until I was so exhausted that I couldn't get up from the floor to do it again. I lay there curled up hugging myself. The tears stopped, and the screaming stopped. I was curled up in a little ball hugging myself, and I felt good.

I was empty of something. Something that had been inside me for a long time. Now I could feel again. I had thought that my feelings were dead, but they were there now. I could feel the pain, the anger, the confusion that had been invisible for so long. I lay curled up in a little ball and fell asleep. A deep, peaceful sleep left me completely rested when I woke up.

I stood up to look out a little window that was completely surrounded by a soft padding that was in the door. There was no one in view and the corridor looked dark. It must be nighttime, and everyone must be asleep. I lay back down on the soft white floor and thought of the newly remembered memories I had. Of feeling the need to run from everything. I felt relief that I could remember. I remembered the lies, the guilt, and the confusion. I remembered a voice preaching to me about my badness. I remembered all of it and felt relief. As I traced the events over the past year, the blanks filled in up until that night when I had sat in the dark waiting for someone to come and help me. After that, I was confused and could not remember. I knew I had been in the hospital but could not remember what had happened here. As I lay down waiting for the day to come, I knew that somehow I had to get out of this horrible place. I knew that I was still confused and needed help, but there had to be another way. Someone else could help me. I had to get out. After hours and hours of trying to think of a way of escaping, I heard the door open and saw Betty coming toward me. When her compassionate expression was close enough for me to see, the tears again began to flow from my eyes. These were quiet tears. "Can I come out now?"

"Oh, yes honey. You stand up now, and I'll untie those sleeves. You just stand still honey." I stood patiently for a short time, and soon my arms fell freely to the sides of my body. It felt good to be able to move them, and I held them up and dropped them down a couple of times as I said, "that sure feels better."

"You feeling O.K. now Deedy?"

"Yes, I think so."

"Come on then, let's get you something to eat. You must be starving."

I followed her out into the brightness of the lighted corridor and into the dayroom where breakfast was being served. The sweet smell of pancakes and eggs filled the air and entered my nostrils making me keenly aware of my newly awakened sense of smell. It had been so long since I had smelled anything that I slowly inhaled the delicious fragrance and was overwhelmed with emotion as silent tears filled my eyes.

The next few days were filled with vivid feelings and sensations of all kinds. I felt sadness as I remembered my Mother crying and wanted the comfort of her warm hug. At times I felt tired, and at times I felt the twinge of hunger pains in my stomach. I felt the refreshing water when I took a bath and the delicious textures of food as it entered my mouth. I felt discomfort and enjoyment. I was glad my memory was back and felt sure everything else would soon be as it should. I remembered Freddy and was grateful that he had not seen me when I was so sick. I felt sadness when I learned that my brother had not been to see me, and warmth when I found out that Daddy had brought me candy. I felt confusion about why I had hurt myself without even knowing it. How could someone do that to themselves? As I looked at my wrists, the lines were a testimony to my attempt at self-destruction.

As the days passed and I talked to Dr. Branscom, I tried to tell her about my feelings but found it hard to talk about. I wanted her help. I knew I needed help. I tried and tried to share my feelings, but couldn't find words to express what was still inside me. We talked about little things such as how I felt toward Mother and Daddy. What I thought about school and the kids and my relationship with Freddy. I didn't tell her we slept together. I didn't tell her about the voice that talked to me about my badness. I didn't know how to tell her about the strangeness I felt. I had the feeling that I was split into two people, one who was good and one who was bad. I didn't tell her about this feeling. I only told her about the surface things, the kind of things that were easy to talk about.

Three weeks had passed since that night when my memory returned and as I followed the nurse back from my sessions with Dr. Branscom, a shadowy idea that had been hiding deep within my mind began to take form. It was useless talking to Dr. Branscom. It was hopeless to continue this way day after day. Nothing was being solved. As I thought about the hours, days, weeks, and months I had spent in this horrible prison, I felt a terrible heaviness that lay within me like some poisonous material. I knew I had to come up with some escape. There had to be some way out of here. I was no longer in the maximum security section of Westerly and had graduated to Building Two where I was allowed some freedom. If I planned carefully, I was sure I could come up with a plan, a way out.

The nurse and I crossed the green lawn and entered Building Two, as I thought about a way to escape. Tomorrow I was scheduled for a shock treatment. Afterward, I would find a way. That night when I was given my medicine, Betty reminded me not to drink anything after midnight. "If you wake up during the night, Deedy, remember don't drink any water. You're scheduled for a shock treatment first thing in the morning."

# Chapter Twenty Two

# Treatment

The treatments had become somewhat routine for me now, and I was not as afraid of them as I used to be. The main difference was that I was always put soundly to sleep. I rolled over on my side and waited for the pink liquid to fill me with that warm floating feeling. I lightly rubbed my index finger back and forth over the ridges and valleys of gray paint on the wall next to my bed. The surface of the wall felt cool against the skin on my finger as I thought about my plan of escape. After tomorrow's shock treatment, when I woke up I would find a way.

"Wake up Deedy. It's time for your medicine." I sat up squinting at the bright light and was surprised that morning was already here, and remembered that today was a shock treatment day.

I got up to go to the bathroom as I asked, "Which doctor is giving the shock treatments today?"

"Dr. Branscom, Dr. Carl, and Dr. Jamison are all out of town to a conference of some kind this weekend, so Dr. Parks is standing in for them. He was here a couple of times last year, but I don't think you were here then."

"Oh. Will he be in to talk to me before they put me to sleep?" Sometimes the doctors that gave shock treatments would come to my room, and we'd talk before I was given my sleeping medicine, and it always made me feel more relaxed just knowing who was doing the treatment.

"I don't know Deedy. It's getting late now, and he hasn't arrived yet. It all depends on how much time there is after he gets here."

"Oh," I replied as I lay back down on my bed to wait for the first medicine so I could feel relaxed.

They gave me three different kinds of medicine before I fell asleep. The first one just made me feel drowsy and relaxed. The second one made it hard for me to move my muscles and made me feel sort of paralyzed. The last one they gave me shortly before the actual treatment and it made me fall asleep immediately. Sometimes before the second medicine, I heard them wheeling in a machine while the nurses put soft cloth straps on my ankles, knees, thighs, arms and abdomen and chest. I could not move my body so much as an inch when they were through. They usually did this when I was asleep after my third medicine, but sometimes they did it after the second one, as I lay awake waiting and watching what they were doing.

Here Deedy, sit up and swallow this." I obeyed swallowing the thick syrupy sweet tasting liquid. Soon the first medicine was flowing nicely through my body and I felt a warm, relaxed sensation.

I shut my eyes and floated in and out of a light sleep when I heard something being rolled in beside my bed and opened my eyes to see who was there. A man in a white coat was standing next to a black box-like machine that had knobs on the front of it. It was about table height and came to the man's waist. I felt a shot go into me with the second medicine as two other nurses came in carrying the cloth straps and began to tie my legs down. I asked when they would give me the last medicine.

"Don't worry Deedy. Lay down and relax."

As I lay down, I began to sense a shadowy fear that was building up in my arms and legs and spreading throughout my body.

"Why haven't you put me to sleep yet?"

"Just relax Deedy." The straps were tight now, and I couldn't move.

"Please give it to me now."

"Relax Deedy."

"Please, I'm scared. Won't you PLEASE put me to sleep NOW?" The fear had spread throughout my entire body and was growing to such a pitch that I could hardly think. My heart was beating in my chest so hard and so fast that it was strangling my lungs, making it impossible to breathe. My throat was thick and dry as I whimpered, "put me to sleep?"

A man's voice said, "Yes Deedy. Don't worry." Something in his voice betrayed him. I didn't believe his words.

I was imprisoned under the straps, and I begged, "PLEASE." I could hear the man moving things at the head of my bed, but could not see what he was doing. I was terrified with fear that flooded my body and burned my head. I was dizzy and could not breathe. My throat was thick to the point of closing. My heart was pumping so fast that I could feel the pulse in my neck as it throbbed with expanding pressure.

"DON'T DO THIS TO ME," I screamed. Silence.

I cried out "PLEASE DON'T" as something was jammed inside my mouth, and my jaw was clamped shut by strong hands. More hands pushed down on my ankles and arms and shoulders as something pressed against the temples of my head. Fear was deafening my ears and constricting my heart.

"NOW" echoed through the room. With sudden swiftness, an ice pick pierced my brain exploding it into millions of jagged pieces of textures, sounds, smells, colors and tastes that flew in all directions. Horrible! Horrible sensations! Lost in dark swirling terror! Fear!

Terror! My brain was helplessly floating within my lacerated skull as it too shattered into billions of shreds. My entire being agonized with convulsive contractions and expansions as my soul collapsed from strangulation and then exploded again and again. I was reduced to a microcosm and buried in an enormously inflated heavy blackness. Consumed. I was gone.

# Chapter Twenty Three
# Westerly Hospital

When I woke up, I did not dare open my eyes or move a single muscle in my body. I wasn't going to let them know I was awake. I hid behind my dark eyelids for the longest time making sure no one else was in the room with me. Silence. Only my breathing. Slowly I opened my eyes to see an empty room. A dim light filtered through the closed blinds giving the impression that it was either dawn or dusk. I was still imprisoned under the tight straps and could not move my body.

I must have slept through the day and now I would have to make up a plan. Never again! I would never again let them force such an awful thing on me! Never! Never! I pushed the nightmare memory of the treatment out of my head, not allowing myself to become a captive of the fear that was encroaching on my feelings, ready to take possession of me again. I took long deep breaths, inhaling, and exhaling, to help myself be the ruler of my emotions. I had to stay calm. I would not let them know I remembered what had happened. I would remain calm and appear happy. I would keep what little freedom they gave me in Building Two. When I had the opportunity, I would flee. It would be soon. I had to escape soon. Very soon.

"Well. Good morning Deedy." Betty walked over to the blinds and opened them letting in the warm morning sun to shine through the window lighting the room.

"Good morning," I returned with smiling lips. "You seem to feel good today," she observed. "What time is it?"

"It's six thirty. Time to rise and shine" she cheerfully replied. "What day is it? When was my shock treatment?"

"Today is Tuesday, and you had the shock treatment yesterday morning. You've had a nice long rest. Now it's time to get up." She released me from the restraints, and I stretched my stiff body as I sat on the edge of the bed. I carefully stepped to the floor and held on while my body got used to being in an upright position. I could feel the blood pulse back down into my legs and through my arms. "Your mother is coming this morning with some new crafts for the ladies. After breakfast, you go on over to the craft building and help her set things up."

"Okay."

Mother had been so unhappy with the hospital's lack of creative activities that she made a tremendous fuss. Dr. Branscom, who was a part owner in Westerly, told Mother that if she wanted to set up a craft workspace, there was an empty outbuilding that was near her office that was not being used. She gave Mother an expense allowance to go and buy the supplies she would need. Now Mother spends two hours four days each week working with the patients in the craft building. The patients in Building Three don't participate since they have to be under maximum security all the time. The patients in my building and Building One take turns each day working on craft projects with Mother. There are not supposed to be more than eight patients in the craft building at any one time. Two or three nurses or aides are always present to help Mother with the patients and they all think Mother is a saint because she devotes so much of her time to her daughter. No one else has any relatives who spend even half the amount of time here that Mother does.

As I ate breakfast, a plan of escape began to form in my mind. Today was the perfect time. Everyone thinks I am so calm and controlled after a shock treatment that they don't watch me very closely. The craft building is across the lawn and fairly near Dr. Branscom's office at the edge of the Westerly Hospital property where there are no fences of any kind. After I eat breakfast and they send me to help Mother that will be the time to escape. Excitement rose inside me at the thought of getting away from here. I would sneak away and call Freddy.

Betty and I had just left my building and were on the front steps when she said, "You go on over there now and help your Mother. I'll stand here on the steps and watch as you cross the lawn. You go quickly, your Mother is waiting."

"Okay." I smiled back as I walked down the steps to the path that led to Dr. Branscom's office and the craft building. I walked casually, humming some unknown tune in my head until I got to the point where I would have to cross over the lush grass to reach the door of the craft building. I could see movement through the open door and knew Mother must be busy setting up the projects she had planned for today. I turned my head and glanced behind me as I stepped onto the grass, and saw

Betty smiling as she watched me. I waved and smiled back as I headed for the opened door. When I was almost there, I again looked back and saw Betty disappear inside Building Two. I stopped and took a deep breath, forcing a controlled calm to fill my body. I looked around making sure no one was watching.

# Chapter Twenty Four

## Escape

I could see Dr. Branscom's car in the parking lot beside her office along with several other cars. Quickly I darted to the side of the craft building and waited a moment to make sure no one had seen me. I ran over the grass and crouched down behind some bushes that grew next to the side of Dr. Branscom's office where there were no windows. I looked around, and no one was in sight. So far so good. After a few seconds, I ran to the parking lot and darted behind the first car to conceal myself while I caught my breath. I could feel my heart beating hard with the excitement I was finding hard to control. I again darted to another car and another until I was at the edge of the parking lot next to the busy intersection of two main highways. The light was green so I quickly ran across to the other side of the street. I waited on the curb for the second light to turn green as I furtively looked back at the parking lot of the hospital. There was still no one in sight; apparently they didn't know I was gone. It took what seemed like an eternity for the light to change as my heart beat faster and faster. I took several deep breaths and swallowed hard to try to force the lump back down my throat and wiped the perspiration off that was beading up on my upper lip and nose. Finally, the light turned green and I flew across the second highway and ran down the sidewalk trying to put as much distance as possible between myself and the hospital before stopping again to look behind me.

After I had gone two blocks, I felt safe enough to stop and check to see if anyone was following. I leaned against a brick wall that was next to a large window with a sign painted on it that read 'FAST - One-day cleaning service.' I looked up and down the block checking the people who were visible while I again took the time to catch my breath. Perspiration was now covering my forehead and trickling from the back of my neck making warm little streams that I could feel winding their way down the center of my back. My blouse was sticking to the damp, clammy skin under my arms and my legs were trembling. I waited for a couple of minutes to try to regain a calm appearance while I decided what to do next. I didn't know anyone who lived close to the hospital and it was too far from Freddy's house to walk so I would have to call him to come and get me.

As I rested against the wall, I realized I couldn't remember Freddy's phone number and looked around to see if I could see a phone booth that might have a telephone book in it. At the end of the block, I saw one and headed for it. I was looking through the pages when a flash of panic shot through me as I remembered I didn't have any money. How was I going to call him? I felt inside the change return cup hoping to find a dime someone had left behind, but it was empty. I pushed open the doors and darted out and down the street further away from the hospital. I remembered there was usually a phone booth every three or four blocks on the main highway and ran looking for another one hoping to find a dime. After running three blocks, I saw one, pushed open the doors and felt into the cup, but no dime. I again ran out and down the street looking for a third booth and repeated the same thing, to no avail. By now, I was so out of breath that I was panting as I held my side trying to relieve the pain that was coming from the cramp in my side.

I sat down on the curb away from the busy highway and tried to come up with some solution to my problem. Tears began to fill my eyes when the thought that only one tiny little dime was left between Freddy's rescue and me. I reached down in the gutter thinking that maybe someone had dropped some money and came up with only one dirty tarnished copper penny. I'd have to look further and stood up wiping the perspiration from my forehead, and ran down another three blocks, pushing open the doors to the booth looking for a dime. No dime! I ran on to another booth and another and another. No dimes! I was panting so fast that I was forced to lean against the outside of the booth as my heart pounded inside my chest. I was now out of the business district and in a residential one. After several minutes, it became easier to breathe as the pounding in my chest slowed down. I looked at the neat, well-manicured lawns that spread out in front of a row of houses that lined both sides of the street. The houses were not large and looked like each other except that each was painted a different color and had different kinds of bushes decorating the front yards. They were friendly looking homes that appeared as though nice people probably lived in them. Maybe, just maybe someone would let me use their phone.

I slid my body down the side of the telephone booth until I was sitting on the sidewalk and rested my back against the wall of the booth. I closed my eyes and silently whispered, "Please God, help me find a way. Let someone nice be home to help me. Please."

Taking several deep breaths, I waited until my heart and lungs felt normal again, then stood up and tried to press the wrinkles out of my blouse and peddle pushers with the palms of my hands. I wiped the perspiration from my upper lip, nose and forehead and out of my eyes where the salty moisture was stinging them. Then I wiped my hands against the sides of my pants to remove the perspiration that was on them. I looked at the row of houses across the street and then at the row on my side of the street, trying to determine which one I should choose. I decided on the white one across the street that was second from the corner and headed for it. I slowly walked up the two steps to the screen door that was in front of the main door and rang the bell.

It seemed like a long time before I heard footsteps and watched as the main door opened. A young boy appeared behind the closed screen, and words came out of my mouth so slowly that it made me sound as though I didn't know what I wanted. "Is.... Your.... Mom ....home? "

"Mom, there's some lady at the door," the boy yelled at some unseen person. A kindly looking, plump women in a flowered print dress came up behind the boy and asked, "May I help you?"

"Well, I lost my dime and need to call someone and was wondering if I could use your phone for just a minute" again my voice betrayed the confident appearance I was trying to project.

"Well, I suppose so. Come on in."

I stepped into the small, homey living room as she pointed over to a telephone that was sitting on a small table next to a plaid couch.

"Oh, I forgot the number I want to call and wondered if you have a telephone book I could use."

"Well," she replied hesitantly, "sit down. I'll have Timmy get it from the kitchen," she said looking at the boy.

I sat on the edge of the couch as she sat in the chair next to it and looked at her watch. "Shouldn't you be in school?"

"Oh, well, um… I was… um… was just… um" I stammered, not able to think of any explanation to give her, as my eyes began to fill up with unwanted tears. Again I tried, "I um… um I, I was just…..I.""" Nothing would come out that made any sense.

"I lost..my…dime……I..um …..just wanted.... um …."

Finally giving up, I bent my head toward my lap to hide the tears that were beginning to slide down my cheeks.

"What's the matter, honey?" No reply, I just couldn't get any of my words out.

"Have you run away? Does your mother know where you are?"

"Oh please help me. I had to run away - it's such an awful place — they do horrible things there — please help me — if I can just call Freddy — he'll come and take me away — please let me use the phone — I have to get away... please help me."

She moved to the couch putting her arm around my shoulder and said, "Now slow down honey. Who does horrible things to you? Where have you run away from?"

"Westerly. That awful hospital! Please help me. They hurt me there and force horrible treatments on me that hurt my brain so much. Please."

"You just sit here for a minute and I'll get you a glass of water. I'll help you, now don't you worry." She disappeared through the door to the back of the house. After several minutes, she returned carrying a tall glass of water and a box of Kleenex.

"Here you wipe your eyes and drink this. You can sit here for a while and rest before you call anyone. You look like you've been running for some time, and I'll bet you're tired."

I pulled a Kleenex out of the box and wiped my eyes and nose, then took the water realizing that my mouth was dry with thirst.

The nice woman sat down next to me again and asked, "How long ago did you run away?"

"This morning."

"Well, you must be tired. You just sit here and rest for a while."

I leaned back against the couch and began to feel more comfortable as the tears finally stopped flowing. Timmy came through the door carrying a telephone book that he handed to his mother, and she then handed it to me saying, "I'll get a pencil and paper so you can write the number down. I'll be back in just a second."

As she got up, the doorbell rang. She pushed Timmy aside as she went toward the door saying, "Timmy you go back to your room now and stay there. I'll call you when you can come out."

She opened the door and two men dressed in white coats and pants that I recognized from the hospital came through the opening toward me so rapidly that I barely had time to jump up and head for the door that led to the kitchen and the back of the house. The men were too quick for me and I felt them grab my arms and shoulders as I tried to flee.

"NO DON'T TAKE ME BACK. Please, please, please,"

"Come on now Deedy, you know you have to come with us. Everyone will be worried about you."

Trying to push and pull myself out of their strong grasp, I looked pleadingly at the woman while whimpering, "You don't understand. It's awful there. It's awful. Please help me. I've got to get away."

There was pity in her eyes as she looked at me as if I was some wounded animal.

Anger flared within me as I suddenly found enough hidden strength to break free from their hold and darted through the door. Before I had reached the sidewalk, they were on top of me with even greater force, one man grabbing tightly around my chest and the other one pulling my legs up in the air knocking me down to the grass covered ground. Within an instant, one of them was sitting on my legs while the other one had forced a coarse white shirt over the front of me pushing my arms in the sleeves and pulling them behind me to tie them so I was hugging myself. I kicked at them and screamed at the lady who was standing at the door watching.

"You don't know what you've done. It's a horrible place. How could you do this!"

The man sitting on my legs said, "Come on now Deedy. Settle down, there's no point in getting nasty. You know you have to come back with us so you might as well cooperate."

All the fight, fire and energy drained out of me, and I slumped down into the arms of the other man in resignation as I realized that there was nothing I could do against two strong men. They carried me to a car that was parked on the street in front of the house and as I looked back I saw the little boy Timmy standing beside his mother who had her arm protectively wrapped around his shoulder.

# Chapter Twenty Five

# Returned To Imprisonment

While I was driven back to the hospital, I stared blankly out of the windows seeing nothing as I despondently thought of what they would do to me when I was returned. I was fairly sure that if put up a fight they would put me back in that padded room and keep my arms tied behind my back. Or maybe they would put me under that rubber sheet in the tub full of ice. I would not put up a fight. Maybe if I seemed calm, maybe they would only give me lots of medicines so I would sleep. I was sure that no matter what I did, they would give me a shock treatment, probably tomorrow. I was also sure they would put me back in Building Three so I couldn't run away again. I sat crumpled up in the corner of the back seat next to one of the men feeling completely alone, knowing no one in the entire world understood what it was like to be locked up and treated the way they treated me. I had tried to tell Mother, but she said they were helping me. I think she truly believed that. When I had told her I was afraid of the ice tub and the shock treatments, she said Dr. Branscom had told her they were very good ways to help a patient calm down and clear away the confusion.

As I sat there trying to think of just one person who would believe me and help me, I was overcome by a feeling of futility. I was still filled with confusion and guilt. I knew I needed help. But not in this awful place. I couldn't tell Dr. Branscom about my secret feelings as she had too much power over me. She was the one who told them to give me shock treatments and to put me in those ice baths. She could do anything she wanted to me, and everyone seemed to think she was doing the right thing. Mother told me she was one of the leading doctors in child psychiatry and had been highly recommended by the police department and by my pediatrician.

How could any of the things she did to me be good? How could they help me get well? It was useless; she could never really help me. We drove past the parking lot and around to the back of Building Three, where two nurses were waiting. As they came toward the door on my side of the car, their faces and white uniforms began to blur through the tears of despair that had pooled in my eyes. I was completely helpless against their power over me. I couldn't resist or they would punish me and I couldn't submit because then it would be even easier for them to do horrible things to me. My body became rigid with fear, and I lost all control over my shaking muscles as they convulsed spasmodically. One of the nurses had a hypodermic needle ready to plunge into my body as the other one opened the door. I did not move or cry out as I sat frozen with fear while the muscles in my body continued to convulse. The needle punctured my skin sending warm flowing sensations through the side of my hip, which quickly spread through all of my body. I was aware of being carried some place as I floated into blackness.

I had no idea how long I lay unmoving beneath the restraints that were all too much a part of my life. My body had no feeling, and I felt as though I wasn't there. My mind was vivid with images and didn't seem to be connected to the body that housed me. I had only one recognizable emotion inside of me, and that was frustration. I tried to remember what had happened since I was returned to the hospital, but could not. The memories within my electrified brain had again been completely scrambled by their so-called treatment that was supposed to shock me back into what they called 'cooperation.' As I tried to hold on to some semblance of order within my thoughts, I was again aware of the tremendous sense of frustration that kept all logical thought from my grasp.

Glimpses of the desire to disappear were mixed with a deep need to live. Images of me as a good girl and as a bad girl became a jumbled mix floating around me. I had not felt like a whole, complete person ever since that awful man had taken me away. Strange, how I was able to remember him even through all the confusion, deceit, hate, and anger within me. I had vague glimpses of myself from long ago before he came and ruined everything. I had been a person who used to laugh and feel pretty and had beautiful dreams. There must be some way to recapture those feelings. There had to be some way to release the treasonous thoughts that were always throwing me into confusion. It seemed all I did now was cry.

I was pretty sure God didn't care what was happening to me. He let that man take me which changed my whole world into a turbulent mess. I wanted to pray to Him but I didn't believe He would want to hear my prayers. Everyone had told me God loves us, but I didn't think He loved me. He's left me alone to figure everything out by myself. I'll pray to Him later and maybe He'll change His mind.

A week or so later, as I lay floating down the gray river of paint on the wall next to me, I thought there must be some way to regain my life. I lay in the silence of what must have been night and wondered how many more times they had sent those electrical charges through my head trying to numb whatever was left inside my skull. I had almost no feeling in my body and no memory of any sequence of events that I might have been a part of. I had a vague recollection of having tried to escape, but could not remember why I had not succeeded.

I had hazy memories of some boyfriend way back somewhere in my past, but could not picture what he looked like or what his name was. I was able to see images of my mother and father, but when I tried to focus on an image of my brother, I could not. I wasn't able to hold on to any imagery of who my friends had been, or if I even had any. I could not remember when I had last been to school or what the house I used to live in looked like. Through the emptiness in my brain, the one image that did appear persistently with graphic clarity was that of having shock treatments. My memory told me with vividness that they were horrible. I lay still and silent for eons, imprisoned under the restraints that had become part of me. Time didn't seem to come in a measurable form. It continued forever with sameness as I lay waiting for the next blow that fate would lay on me. If there is a God where is He? How could these horrible things happen to me if God is real?

I tried to move my fingers, but could not even feel where they were. I had a vague memory of hearing voices singing Christmas carols and wondered if Christmas had slid by me or if I only remembered some Christmas from long ago. I lay there waiting and wondering.

"Deedy. Deedy, wake up. Wake up now." I saw a face peering down at me and wondered whose it was.

"Come on now, wake up. That's right open your eyes." I saw two faces in front of my opened eyes.

"That a girl. It's time to wake up Deedy." The two faces joined, and again there was only one face peering down at me.

"Come on Deedy. You keep your eyes opened now. It's time to wake up." My eyes didn't want to stay opened, and slowly they shut again.

"Deedy! Deedy! You wake up. You hear me. Wake Up. Wake up."

For some reason, someone wanted me to wake up.

"It's a wonderful sunny morning. That's a good girl. Now you keep those eyes opened. We want to get you out of bed, so you have to stay awake. That's right. Keep them opened."

Someone was removing the restraints that had become part of me, and someone else was rubbing my legs. I was starting to feel them now, and the rubbing felt good. There was a tingling sensation inside my fingertips as I wiggled them in their mittens. My back began to have feeling as I reached my arms above my head and stretched my body to relieve the stiffness. Looking around, I recognized the gray walls that surrounded me, as one of the nurses walked over to the closed blinds, opened them and then left the room.

"How do you feel Deedy?" I wasn't sure how to answer since I was just barely beginning to feel anything. "You feel okay honey?" The voice that came from the dark skinned face had a familiarity about it that made me think I must know the nurse who stood in front of me. She looked at me with a kind, compassionate expression that gave me the feeling that we were friends.

"What's your name?"

"Betty. Honey, my name is Betty."

"I remember you. I remember you're nice and I remember liking you."

"Yes, Deedy. We are good friends. Now I want you to sit up slowly." Slowly I raised my head and shoulders while pushing my body up against the mattress with my arms. After I pushed half way up, I rested on my elbows for a moment and then continued up until I was sitting.

"That a girl. How does it feel?"

"Fine, but I can't believe how stiff I am."

"You'll be fine. Just you sit there for a few minutes while I get you some water to drink."

"Okay." While I was waiting for her to return, I moved my legs to the edge of the bed and reached for the floor with my feet. I held on to the bed as I transferred my weight from the bed to my legs. I stood for a few seconds when slowly I felt the floor begin to disappear from underneath me. I reached for the table that was next to the bed, but all I felt was a jarring blow to my jaw as my body slumped to the floor.

"Oh no! Deedy! What have you done now?" I looked up at her

expression of disbelief as I lay motionless on the cold linoleum floor.

"I didn't mean to fall. I thought I could walk."

"You just lay there for a second. You hear me! You lay still!! I'll be right back! DO NOT try to get up! Just lay there and YOU WAIT for me to come back!" She ran to the closet and grabbed some towels that were on the shelf and came back to me quickly bending down and pressing a towel against my chin.

"You hurt any place else Deedy?"

"No. I don't even feel anything. I'm fine."

"No, you ain't. Somehow you've managed to cut your chin wide open. Now you lay still and let me see what else you've hurt."

She bent down even closer and examined my legs, picking each one up and moving it first at the ankle, then at the knee and asked, "How does that feel?"

"I'm fine. I'm okay. Really I am."

"You don't go telling me how fine you are. Just you let me do the checking." She then proceeded to move each arm the way she had done with my legs and asked, "How's that feeling Deedy?"

"Fine. Really."

"Well, maybe. Now let's take a closer look at that chin of yours." She put her face very close to mine, and I could smell a sweetness that came from her skin. "That's pretty deep. I think you'll need a couple of stitches Deedy. But first, let's get you up off that floor. You sit up slowly and hold on tight to me and I'll do the moving. Do you hear?"

"Okay." I sat up and she lifted my hands to her shoulders, then put her arms tightly around to my back, pressing her body against mine she firmly lifted me with a strength that was concealed within her delicate feminine body. Before I could even try to help her, I found myself planted securely on the mattress as she raised the metal bars that were attached to the sides of my bed. I guess she was making sure I wouldn't try that again.

"Just making sure you don't pull that on me again!" I smiled as she again pressed the towel against my chin.

"I'll go see if Dr. Carl's still here. I saw him earlier this morning and maybe he can close that cut up for you. You hold this tightly against your chin and stay lying down. I'll be right back." She turned and left the room as I pushed the towel against the cut. It didn't hurt, and I thought she was making something out of nothing, but I stayed still and waited for her return.

Within minutes she walked through the open door with a tall, slim silver haired man following close behind her. He leaned over the metal bars on my bed pulling his small wire-rimmed glasses down so they rested on the end of his nose and said, "Well, let's see what we have here," while he tilted my chin up and peered at the cut.

Looking up at him I said, "I don't think it's very bad."

Ignoring my comment he said, "This will need a few stitches." Clearing his throat, he turned to Betty saying, "I want you to go get me a local anesthetic. Go and see if it's in the back room. I'd like one-percent Xylocaine with epinephrine. If not, just bring what local anesthetic is there. Also, bring me some catgut and silk sutures."

Then he turned back to me saying, "Well, now young lady how did you do this?"

"I was just trying to stand up, but I fell, and I guess my chin hit that table," I replied pointing to the table that was pushed a little way out from the side of the bed. "It doesn't hurt. Really."

Betty returned and spread out a light blue paper towel on the table and set a box that held some silver instruments next to a hypodermic needle she put on the towel. Alongside the instruments, she put several cotton swabs, some gauze, and white medical tape, and what looked like a pair of thin white rubber gloves. After she had arranged everything to her satisfaction, she pushed the table closer to where the doctor was standing and lowered the bars on the side of my bed.

"Is it going to hurt?" I asked the doctor as I watched him stretch the tight rubber gloves over his hands.

He stopped what he was doing and looking directly into my eyes as the corners of his mouth formed a half smile in his gently lined face giving him an expression of compassionate concern. He adjusted his glasses so they were even further down to the very tip of his nose as he replied, "You might feel a slight pulling sensation when I inject the anesthetic, but that should be all. I will numb the area before putting the sutures in. You let me know if you feel anything."

Something about his manner was reassuring and gave me a sense of confidence and trust. I tried to relax as he gently rubbed a cool, moist cotton swab over the wounded area. Next, he picked up the needle, and I felt its sharpness as it punctured the skin on my chin to inject the first dose. Then he moved it to another spot and another, which by now I could not feel. I began to relax when I realized I really would not feel his needle as he was sewing up the cut.

As he worked to suture my chin, I closed my eyes and again wondered what time of the year it was and if I had missed Christmas. It wasn't long before I heard his voice say,

"There you are, young lady. We'll leave the gauze on it for a couple of days and by next Monday, the stitches should be ready to come out. How does it feel?"

"Fine. I don't even feel it."

"Good. Now don't you try to get up again unless Betty or someone else is right here by your side. You understand?"

"Yes. I thought I could walk by myself."

"Well, now you know! So don't try that again!" His warm smile softened the harshness that came from his orders, and I smiled back.

After he left and Betty had cleared everything from the table, she again helped me as I sat on the edge of the bed. This time she did not leave from my side as I got used to the change from laying down.

"What time of the year is it?"

"It's January Nineteenth Deedy."

"You mean I missed Christmas?"

"Well, we had Christmas carolers and your mother and daddy were here, and even your brother came to visit you. But you weren't feeling so good at that time and maybe you don't remember."

"Was there a Christmas tree?".

"Oh yes! Your mother helped the ladies make all kinds of pretty things that they hung on a nice big green tree. We had presents underneath it and everything. Your mother helped the ladies make pretty gifts that they exchanged with each other on Christmas morning. Yes, it was a regular old fashion Christmas around here! We had turkey, stuffing and all kinds of sweet goodies. Your mother and daddy brought a big box of fancy Christmas cookies she said she got from the Swedish Bakery. They were real tasty and just as pretty as could be. We all had ourselves a fine time!"

"Funny, I don't remember it. I sort of remember hearing carolers, but that's all."

"Well, honey, you've had a rough time and lots of shock treatments. You'll remember everything soon. Don't you worry about it. When the time is right those memories will just pop right back into your head. Now let's walk a while to get some strength back in those legs of yours."

"Has Mother been here?"

"Yes. She's been here to see you every day that you didn't have a treatment. And she's coming this afternoon right after lunch. So let's get you moving so you'll be ready for her when she arrives."

I was sitting in the day room when she walked in and put her arms around me holding on for a very long time. She pulled back and looked at me saying, "How does that feel?"

"I don't really feel it. It hurts a little to move my jaw, but not that much."

"Did they take an X-ray?"

"No. Dr. Carl just sewed it up."

She closely examined my face again and said, "It doesn't look right. Something looks like it's not lined up right. I think you should have an X-ray. I'll go talk to the head nurse. You wait here; I'll be back in a minute."

After a short time, she returned with the head nurse following her. Mother took my face in her hands gently touching my jaw by my ear and said, "Look. Something is wrong right here. This doesn't look right. I want her to have an X-ray."

The nurse replied. "We'd have to take her down to Community Hospital since we don't have that kind of equipment here and she's scheduled for a shock treatment tomorrow morning. Maybe I can talk to Dr. Branscom and see if we could take her day after tomorrow."

"No. I want her to have one today. There is something wrong with her jaw. You go talk to Dr. Branscom now, and if I have to I'll drive her over for the X-rays myself."

"Dr. Branscom has left for the day. I'll see if I can get her on the phone and tell her what you want. I'll be back soon, you wait here with Deedy."

After much discussion and a lot of fuss on my mother's part, they agreed to let her drive me over with a male attendant to get the X-ray.

A vague sense of exhilaration pushed through the blandness of my feelings at the thought of going away from Westerly, even if it was to another hospital, and even if it was for only a short time. We stepped out into the bright sunshine and I looked up to see the clear blue sky. It was such a bright blue and so vivid that I instinctively shut my eyes to shield myself from the overpowering reality that hit me. I was finally going to leave this dreadful place. I would have to come back I knew, but at least I was leaving for now.

The sound of seagulls reminded me that outside of my imprisonment there was life. I looked around and saw some graceful white seagulls flying to some destination that only they knew. The air surrounding me was alive with sounds. Birds chirped back and forth to each other and insects buzzed, making music. My body felt like it was floating through the vividly real life that I was viewing. It was as though I was watching a movie that caused sensations deep within me. I could smell the warm fragrance of freshly cut vegetation that mingled with the saltiness that was blowing from the sea air that was two blocks away. It didn't seem two blocks away. It seemed as though I was standing on the sand next to the surf and could feel the sea spray on my skin. The intensely living beauty of the day filled my head with a wonderful lightness and made me want to be a part of the world outside of the prison where I had been forever. It was as though someone had pulled up a shade, which had covered the windows of my eyes for a lifetime. There was so much life all around me that I felt overwhelmed by it. There was the sound of cars and people moving around as if they were parts of a huge world. I wanted to move with them instead of alone as I had done for so long. What I was seeing made me think maybe there was a God who created all the life I was viewing. Maybe if I asked Him to help me again He would respond this time. I wanted to become a piece of the world that surrounded me and to fit securely in the right spot. As I looked around at life, I suddenly became aware of an intense need to join in with the world and to feel God's presence.

It was like I saw a train moving by me and I felt it was my time to jump on and travel with it. For the first time in what was an eternity, the darkness of the pain-ridden world did not seem so dark anymore. As I looked up and around, I was aware of a distinct separation between me and the panorama encircling me. I was forever the observer, but what I was observing this time was different from anything my memory could recall. Maybe God was really here and I could become a regular part of everything I was seeing. Maybe He was going to let me join the world. I didn't think He would actually help me, but if I became strong enough maybe He'd let me join a world with no confinement or torture.

All the way to the hospital I felt as though I was watching a spiritual movie. It was the kind of movie where God reached down and made people feel good inside. A film that took the viewer into the screen to become a part of the story that featured God as the star. The story flowing passed the windows of the car jumped through the transparency of the glass and flowed into me. It was bright, clear and overflowing with life.

When we arrived, I was able to carry the feeling with me. The reels of the movie were still running. It didn't matter that we had to wait nearly an hour before the X-rays were taken. It gave me more time to absorb the movie and what it meant to me. When the doctor came in to tell mother that my jaw was broken in two places, I thought he must be talking about someone else because I had no pain within me. He said something about one break going through the root of a front tooth and one going through the joint in my jaw. I felt no pain so what he said seemed to be about someone else. Surely a broken jaw would hurt.

"Deedy, come, follow me and I will wire your jaw closed so it will heal properly." The doctor smiled as he took my arm and led me down the corridor.

"How will I eat? How will I talk?"

"You will be on a liquid diet while it's wired. Don't worry about food. You can get plenty of nutrition through a straw. In fact, I've had patients who have gained weight from all the milkshakes and malts while their jaws were wired shut. As far as talking, I'm sure you'll manage." A hearty laugh came from deep inside of him after he spoke. I felt elated as the vibrations from his laughter penetrated into me and made me laugh with him.

Chapter Twenty Six

# The Blessed Break

Lying down on a bed, I let him fix my mouth as dreams of the world outside rolled passed my closed eyelids. I would have a chance to live outside in the real world. I knew I would. I would find where I fit into the outside world. I knew I would. They won't help me, but maybe this time I will be able to mend my life myself. I still felt angry at God for allowing awful things to happen. I'm still fairly sure He doesn't care what happens to me and I have to restore myself all alone. But I'll try to ask Him again for help and see if anything happens.

But if I get no answer and I still don't believe He cares, it will be my responsibility to get myself out of the world I've been forced into for too long. My mind was so empty of private memories that I could think of no one person who would help me. I knew I was alone and that I would have to find my own place myself. I was an observer in the movie of my life, with no script to refer back to, but that was okay. It would be up to me to write the script for myself. They had erased the previous writings with the constant shock treatments. Now the rest of the movie was up to me. I could use the erasure and wipe away what I did not like and write and rewrite until the story was complete. I would be the star, and the plot would be happy and maybe God would enter my world. As the doctor finished wiring my jaw shut I felt the muscles in my cheeks fight their way through the restraints to smile. The smile privately stretched from one side of my face to the other.

"You're smiling Deedy," the doctor observed.

"I feel happy. Why doesn't it hurt?"

The words sounded surprisingly clear as they squeezed through my teeth that were locked so tightly together.

"I have a list of the drugs you have had over the past twenty-four hours, and I think the sedatives have dulled your sense of pain. I'm sure you'll feel it after the drugs have worn off."

On the way back to Westerly, I again viewed the movie that rolled past the glass as I looked out the windows of the car. I could not remember anything that was behind me except that I had once been raped and hurt by an awful man and God had not rescued me. No one had ever known what that did to me because I had never been able to tell anyone. I remembered thinking there were two of me inside fighting. One was good and one was bad. I was sure no one but me knew about this. That was also okay because I was sure no one else could understand since they hadn't experienced what I had been through. I didn't even understand it. But I could live with both the good and the bad because the thoughts from both were my thoughts.

The memories that were vivid to me were connected with the hospital and with the people who worked there. I remembered trying to run away. I also remembered trying to take my life, well maybe not my whole life. Maybe all I tried to do was to get rid of the part of me that I thought was bad. I don't even know what bad means. Someone who's been raped or someone who's had sex without being married? Someone who lies? Someone who is confused and doesn't understand what other people want? I was sure I was not whatever bad was. I knew me better than anyone else and I was the one who had been hurt. It did not happen to anyone else so how could anyone else decide whether or not I was bad? I would rewrite the script for my life and survive.

When we arrived back at Westerly, I told myself that I would do whatever they wanted, so they would see me cooperating and call me 'well.' Then Dr. Branscom would send me home. Somehow I would wait for whatever amount of time they kept me and I would survive. I would not become like some of the patients who acted like they were crazy. I would grab onto something inside myself and pull myself out of the depths I had fallen into. I would survive. I was a piece of some huge puzzle already cut into shapes, and I would find out for myself where my piece fit. Maybe I could not erase the part of the script that was already written, but I could write another page that would be happy and would make the sad pages not seem so sad after all.

We walked into the main entrance, passed by the locked doors, passed the bars dividing the outside from the inside and walked to the desk where someone with some authority decided whether or not a person would be admitted inside or released outside. We were allowed inside and passed by the small room with the locked door next to the office where mysterious medicines were doled out. The medicines were given to patients so they would not feel anything or be able to think about anything. We walked down the empty, harsh colorless corridor where puppet-like patients floated back and forth all day long. We went into the room where I was supposed to live. Into a room that was lifeless, colorless, empty of any clue as to who lived in it. It was void of pictures or anything else that might reflect a sense of feelings. I looked at the bed where I had been tied down many times, tied to the whiteness of the coarse sheets and covered up with the whiteness of a tidy, sterile blanket. Everything was in proper order in the room. There was not much to be out of order, no books, no vases, no decorations were allowed in this room where I had spent hour after hour.

This room was part of the environment where I was supposed to get well. I was supposed to find some reason to want to live while surrounded by this empty environment. Someone somewhere had decided that a patient should be surrounded by an orderly sense of nothingness. Well, I would get well anyway and I would get out of this prison. After just coming back from seeing a glimpse of the living world and the brightness of real life, I was determined I'd be joining that world. They could do with my body whatever they felt they had to do, and I would not fight them because they held the key to the door to my life. They could tie me down, give me drugs, force electricity into my brain and bury my body in ice, but I would not let them enter into my script. What they did to me would only affect my body. I would hold the pen that would finish my story, and I would be the one who would survive in it.

"Deedy, you rest now. You have been through a lot." The voice filtered through my thoughts and reminded me that I was back in my world of incarceration. No discussion. I thought as I lay myself down on the unyielding mattress. No dissension. No argument. No anger. I would be the most agreeable patient they had ever had. They would soon hand me the key to the door.

Mother bent over and took me in her arms sharing the warmth of her body with me. She was a gentle person and so loving to me. My arms responded to hers and soon we were both holding each other in a way that spoke of forgiveness and love. She would be with me the day they gave me the key.

"I don't think they will be able to give you any shock treatments while your teeth are wired." Her words hit me like some wonderful and glorious gift. I had not even thought about that!

As long as my mouth was wired closed, they could not enter my brain with their electricity and stir it into nothingness. The door to my brain was safely wired shut protecting whatever memories might be left in my mind. I would make myself well before they took off the wires. Tears began to fill my eyes, and I held even tighter to Mother. She responded by holding me even tighter. Soon she was almost rocking me in her arms to some unheard melody. Her love for me reinforced my knowledge that I would survive.

The next six weeks went by very slowly, but I was the perfect patient. Dr. Branscom told Mother that she was amazed by the change that had come over me, and she attributed it to the possible shock that might have taken place when my jaw broke. She had no idea that I was determined to get away from her power over me and from the confinement where she kept me.

During my sessions with her in the little cottage at the edge of the property, we talked about forgiveness and understanding. I forgave those who didn't understand what had happened to me, and I even forgave that awful man, thinking he was too sick to even know what he had done. We talked about getting along with people in the world outside and of finding a place for me within that world. She told both Mother and me that I would have to take medicine the rest of my life, or I might become sick again. She tried to tell me that I should have at least one shock treatment a month for the rest of my life so I could keep my thoughts straight. She said some very important people in the business community did just that. They came in on a Saturday morning, had a treatment and left on Sunday and reported to work on Monday morning. She said it helped keep them balanced under the pressures of their lives. She said bank presidents and other important people with great responsibilities came in as outpatients for these treatments. What she said did not seem believable, and I knew that I would not follow her advice, but I didn't reveal this to her.

I just smiled and said, "Oh really."

When I discussed this with Mother, she said, "Well, we'll see. I find it hard to believe that you will be having shock treatments the rest of your life. We will just have to wait and see. You certainly seem to be doing fine without them now."

At night when I climbed into bed and buried myself beneath the course white sheets, a sense of loneliness swept through my body. I was sure I was alone in my battle to get out. But I also knew I would be successful. But how, how would I ever make it? I had no one I could talk to, really talk too. Talking was something I had learned to do a lot of, but it was often false talk. I usually only said what I thought others wanted to hear. Never what was deep inside of me. I wanted to share the things I hid from others, but they would never understand. I tried to talk to God again and asked Him if He was real to please give me the strength to win my battle to get out of this horrible place and live a normal life. I turned to the gray wall by my bed feeling alone.

The gray rivers of paint caught my eye, and as I floated down through the layers of grayness, my sense of being alone overwhelmed me. But through the veil of loneliness I felt positive I was never going to come back to Westerly after I would be released.

Betty or some other night nurse came in with my nightly medicine, and I gratefully swallowed the pink liquid and lay down anxiously waiting for the weightless release it gave me. Night after night, the same routine, the same lonely emptiness. Soon the wires would be coming off my teeth, and I was afraid the shock treatments would begin again. Since my jaw had been wired shut, everything had gone so well. I just wanted it to stay that way, no more treatments ever. I closed my eyes and still felt that lonely sense of having no one. There were so many people who seemed to care what happened to me, but each one of them wanted certain things from me. Dr. Branscom wanted me to be calm and to cooperate with everyone. Mother wanted me to be happy. Daddy wanted me to be good. I pushed all the people out of my thoughts, they just made me feel lonelier. I opened my eyes and moved back into the grayness of the rivers of paint on the wall. As I floated down through the weaving pattern, nothing was important. I could just float. The heavy feeling I had when I thought about my family and all the things that had gone wrong lifted from me and in its place was a weightlessness that could carry me anywhere.

I woke up to see a bright streak of sunshine sneaking through the closed blinds bringing with it a sense of warmth. How long had I been here? It seemed like an eternity. By now I must have missed so much school that I would never graduate. Had it been a year or twenty years, or maybe just weeks? There was no way to tell how much time passed. Each day was the same as the day before it and the day after. Nothing changed, nothing moved on. Morning would come, and it was time to shower and dress. Each patient had to make their bed and tidy up their room. This was strange because there was never anything out of place, but we still went through the motions of 'tidying up.' Next came breakfast in the day room where everyone would congregate. Some of us talked about the food, but most of us said nothing. There were some women who carried on conversations with themselves, about what I don't know. None of the talking ever made much sense. A few of the ladies seemed friendly and smiled at each other. Now and then a familiar face would be missing because one of the lucky ones who got 'well' had gone home. And then a new face would appear as someone had joined us to get well. After breakfast, the patients would stay in the day room where there was a small black and white television. The picture that was on all the time displayed a black, gray and white picture that often as not was just zigzagging lines across the screen. If there was a nurse out in the patio, we could go there and try to get some sun on the pasty white skin we all had.

I had never been so white in all my life; never had I been inside a building for such a long, long time. I ached for the feel of the sun warming my skin while I lay on soft, warm sand. But that was a faraway dream. Some day. Someday. On days when the weather was nice, we would go for a walk out in front of the building where the lawn was so perfectly manicured, but that was only when Betty was on duty. She seemed to be the only nurse who thought that being outside was a good idea. Most of the nurses didn't want to make the effort to go outside with us, or maybe they were afraid one of us might try to escape. The next activity that took place during the day was our noon meal; a large meal usually consisting of meat, potatoes, gravy, bread, peas or corn, salad and some pudding or jello. Occasionally we got cookies or cake. The food tasted the same each day, bland and gray. Now and then we would have a change of pace when they served spaghetti and tomato sauce. On special occasions, we would be served turkey, but that was rare. All the food tasted as though it had been cooked for hours and hours and all the vegetables must have come out of cans because they always looked pale and soggy. After the large noon meal, we went back to our rooms and took naps. The blinds would be drawn tightly shut to block the afternoon sun, and we were supposed to sleep. Sleep was what we did the most; long nights of sleep and then daily naps. Tiredness was something everyone felt all the time. I didn't understand how we could be so tired all the time when we did nothing to get tired. The rest of the day we again did nothing. When I try to think of how the time was filled I have no answer. We did not do anything, except when Mother came.

I suppose I'm one of the luckier ones because Mother visited almost every day for several hours after I'd had my nap. Most of the people here didn't ever have visitors. Everyone said Mother was wonderful. She still set up and guided us with crafts four days each week, and that was the only special activity that we ever participate in. If she didn't bring us arts and crafts, we would have absolutely nothing to do ever. Mother also bought me books to read which was very special. There were no books at the hospital, and the only reading material available to us was an odd assortment of ancient magazines in the day room with ripped or missing covers and pages. As I lay in bed watching the shining dots of dust dance in a sliver of the sunshine that was still sneaking through the blinds, I longed for something, anything to fill up the day I was facing. I was sure I would soon be out of this place, but somehow I had to wade through whatever time was left before freedom came to me.

The days were getting longer for me now that I had become more alert and was not subjected to the shock treatments. Time dragged. Each minute took up hours of time and each hour took days. Afternoon and night blurred into one long sleeping time with hazy hours of eating and walking with reading squeezed in.

Mother had started bringing school work for me to do each day, and she said maybe I wouldn't have to fail my grade if we worked really hard. She had talked to the principal, and there were several subjects that they were not going to make me take to graduate into the twelfth grade. They told her they were going to advance me if I just completed one English course, a civics class and some kind of science class, along with my art classes with Mrs. Brown. Mother had all the books, including one on physiology. The reason she picked physiology for my science course was because the teacher told her that they drew lots of pictures of different parts of the body and did not use math. She thought I would enjoy drawing the pictures. The rest of my credits would be made up with home economics and gym. Maybe with Mother's help, the endless hours left for me at Westerly could be filled with schoolwork and maybe everything would work out. Maybe I could move up with the rest of the class. I thought about the kids that I had been in school with. So many faces had become blurred and so many names were gone from my memory. Mother had brought the school yearbook to try to help me remember, but most of the faces remained nameless pictures. Very few brought back any memories. Those shock treatments had wiped so much from my brain.

# Chapter Twenty Seven

# Missing Memory

I didn't believe I'd ever remember most of it even though Dr. Branscom said my memory would return. There were too many huge blanks. I had no memory of my life before that awful man came. He was the one thing that had remained solidly in my memory right down to his smell and the feel of his skin under my nails, and the pulling of his greasy hair. It was so frustrating to continue having such a clear picture of him while I couldn't remember what life had been like before he came.

Mother told me over and over of long ago happenings. She told me of the time I was a flower girl for the woman who lived in our apartment next to the garage and took care of us when Mother and Daddy went out together. Her name was June and I had adored her. She also told me of the gardener named Curly who lived in a house on our property. She said I also adored him and wanted to play at his house in the back of our property, but Mother said I couldn't. She also told me about times spent at the zoo, about trips our family had taken to Ensenada, Mexico and New York, and about the many times we had taken the train to San Francisco to visit a family friend, who we called 'Aunty Gail.' Aunty Gail always sent me funny birthday gifts of old handmade handkerchiefs with flowers embroidered on them. Mother also described the sights we had seen in Washington D.C. and of many trips we had taken to various places in California. She told me about swimming in the ocean when we visited Bambi in Laguna Beach. I listened. She talked. No memories about her stories came back. I had no history to remember. She told me of the friends I had in school and of the girl who had lived next door and how she and I spent hour after hour playing dolls. She described birthday parties we had in the backyard with loads of kids attending. She described costumes she had made for me to wear during the Halloween celebrations that took place each year in my grammar school.

None of this was real to me, just stories. If I had participated in all the things she described, it had to have been during a different life. There was no memory of any of the things she described. To me they were not things I had participated in. They were gone from my memory. My mind was nothing but a blank wall that I could not pass through. A blank wall had separated me from my past. I could not reach the other side to discover the events that I had lived through. Would I ever remember any of what she described? Would I ever have a life to recall before he came and wiped so much from me? It was nice to hear Mother's stories since they always sounded like such fun; they were good stories, and they touched me, but it didn't feel like I had been part of them.

The future was what I had to concentrate on. Now it would be whatever was in front of me that was important. Would I be able to go back to school and have friends? Would I always be 'the girl who was raped and got sick?' Every now and then the thought of God would pass through my mind, but then I dismissed it. I still didn't believe He cared about me.

"Okay girl, that's enough day dreaming for now. You get up and get some life into you!" Betty's voice penetrated my thoughts. I turned away from the gray rivers on the wall to see Betty's smiling face looking down at me. A pleasant, warm feeling filled me when Betty spoke. She cared about the women in this awful place, and she tried to make friends with everyone. All the other nurses looked down upon us and made us feel like useless beings. Betty really cared. It showed on her face and could be heard in her voice. Sometimes when she was especially proud of something one of us did, she would give a big warm hug.

With Betty's big smile facing me, she said "Today you're getting those wires off your teeth, now you get up and get ready."

"Who's taking me to get them off?"

"Why, your Mother will be taking you. Now get up."

"What time are we going?"

"Right after lunch. She'll be coming around one and your appointment is for one-thirty. I bet it will feel real good getting them off."

"I just hope they don't start giving me shock treatments again. They ruin my memory so much. I need to remember things if I'm going to get out of the eleventh grade. Do you think they'll give them to me?"

She looked thoughtfully at me directing her focus into my eyes and spoke very softly, "Well, Deedy, I can't say, but you sure seem to be doing real great without them."

I finally pulled myself from the bed and stretched my back up as straight as it would go. Walking over to the cabinet where my clothes were folded away, I thought about what I would wear. I wanted this to be a very special day, and I wanted to look as good as I possibly could. Carefully I chose my light blue slacks and dark blue sweater knowing blue was my best color. I would put my hair in a ponytail with several pretty ribbons tied around into a long bow.

After dressing, eating breakfast, waiting and then eating lunch, I went to the door to watch for Mother to come. I waited for what seemed like hours when finally her figure came into view walking down the walk from the parking lot.

"She's here. She's here!"

Betty was standing a little behind me as I spoke. "Now don't you get yourself into a tizzy over this Deedy. You keep calm."

"I will Betty. Don't worry. I'm just so glad. Now maybe they'll let me go home."

"Wait a minute. Anybody say anything about you going home?"

"No. But I've been doing so well and now with the wires off, maybe they will let me go." I want to go so much, and I've been doing everything they want me to do so maybe I will get to go home."

"Well, maybe you will. I'll keep my fingers crossed for you honey." The door opened, and Mother stepped in and gave me the usual big hug and warm kiss on my cheek. I responded with a return hug.

"Are you ready Deedy?" Mother asked as she drew away holding me at arms length with her hands on my shoulders and inspected my dress and hair. "You look nice darling," she said with a smile.

"Thank you Mother. I'm ready. Let's go." We stepped outside into the fresh warm spring day, and I turned to Betty asking, "Isn't someone from the hospital coming with us?"

"No honey, you've been doing so well that they feel you can be trusted to behave yourself with your Mother. Now you run along, and I'll be waiting to see those pretty white teeth again."

As Mother drove me to the Community Hospital, I was filled with a mixture of excitement, fear, and anticipation. What if they didn't let me go home? What if they started giving me more shock treatments? During the entire six weeks that I had the wires on I had not felt any pain in my jaw. But then my mind had been so absorbed with trying to get 'well' and do everything everyone wanted that I couldn't think of much else.

I had managed to work my way back to the last building, and Dr. Branscom has often mentioned how impressed she was with my improvement. I went along with everything she suggested and acted as though I was content with everything. Sometimes it was very hard to put on such a front because my feeling for Dr. Branscom was still full of fear. I don't think she ever knew my true feelings because I'd gotten so good at acting out whatever she and the nurses wanted. My true feelings were buried deep down inside only to be known by me. When we walked into the hospital, the same doctor who had put the wires on was walking out of the building. He stopped and asked how I was doing.

"Fine. Aren't you going to take my wires off today?" I asked timidly.

"No. Dr. Smith is on duty now, and he will be taking them off. I'm glad to see you looking so well." He said as he walked toward the parking lot. I wasn't very happy with the idea of a different doctor taking them off. But then, like everything else, I had no choice in what happened.

We entered the outpatient area, and Mother checked me in at the desk while I sat down to wait. The waiting room was filled with mostly old people and kids with runny noses. Everyone looked miserable. We waited and waited while one person after another took their turn and went in for their appointment. We waited and waited. After one and one-half hours, my name was finally called. By this time, the anxiety in me had built up to a strong pitch. I had trouble sitting still. As I curled my toes inside my shoes pressing them against the floor, all I could think of was to run out of the building and away from everyone I knew.

Hearing my name almost made me jump out of the chair. Somehow I managed to hide my true feelings and appear calm, at least I thought I did. We went into the room where the wires would be removed. It was the same room that the wires had been put on.

"Hello, Deedy. My name is Dr. Smith and I'll be taking the wires off your teeth today. Sit here in this chair and make yourself comfortable. This will only take a few minutes, and it won't hurt a bit." I felt a slight pull against my teeth and heard a snip, snip. Then it was over I could open my mouth, which felt stiff. I tried to open it wide which felt like I was doing something my mouth had never done before. It was the strangest feeling, as though it had never opened.

"It will be a little stiff for a while, but that will be gone within a couple of hours. Don't overdo the stretching. Just open your mouth wider gradually. Don't forget it's been wired shut for some time now and the feeling of opening it will take a little getting used to."

"It sure does feel strange," I replied as I gently exercised my jaw, opening my mouth a little at a time.

"You shouldn't have any trouble." Then looking at Mother he said. "If there is any pain or problems, just have the hospital give us a call." Then he pulled off the thin rubber gloves he had on and dropped them into the waste basket.

Mother and I left and while we were walking to the car I was opening and closing my mouth.

"Mother, do you think Dr. Branscom will let me come home now that the wires are off?"

"I don't know Deedy. You sure seem fine to me. But it's up to her." "Will you ask her, please?"

"I have an appointment with her day after tomorrow and I will be asking what her plans are for you."

"Oh Mother, I so badly want to come home. I still hate this place, and I've been here for such a long time. It seems like a whole lifetime to me. I want to live like other people. I just know I can. Please tell her you think I can go now. You can trust me. I'll be good. I promise. Please."

"Darling, we want you home. But it's up to Dr. Branscom. You know that."

# Chapter Twenty Eight

# Return To Living

Two weeks had passed by fairly quickly now that I was sure I would be free from the horrible place where I had lived for what seemed like a lifetime. Dr. Branscom told Mother I was surprisingly better and would probably be released soon. The thought of being home gave me a wonderfully warm feeling. That's all I could think of and was positive I would never return to Westerly ever again. Dr. Branscom said she was baffled by the recovery that appeared after my jaw was broken and suspected the change may have been precipitated by the injury, but she wasn't sure. I think it was because I couldn't have shock treatments the entire six weeks while my jaw healed. I still enjoyed the feeling the pills gave me and was delighted that they didn't stop them. Since the wires were removed from my teeth, I did have one shock treatment, because Dr. Brandscom said she wanted to be sure the change in my behavior remained.

"We're going to miss you when you're gone from here and I'm going to pray you never return," Betty commented as she sat on my bed watching me get ready to be released.

"I'll miss you too Betty, but nothing else about this awful place. I'm so excited to be out of here and can't wait to start my real life all over again. I just hope my memory starts to work better. I guess I've got a lot of things to discover all over again."

Betty stood up responding with, "I'll also pray your memory returns real soon," as she hugged me very tight.

I finished packing all my belongings just as Mother walked into the room. She hugged me saying "We're so happy you are coming home where you belong."

All the way home I felt my life at Westerly had been unreal, a confinement in a nightmare. Now I was anxious to move into a real existence and to become my own master.

When I saw my home as Mother drove into the driveway towards the garage, I felt full of excitement. I was concerned that my world might get complicated since I couldn't remember anything about my previous life. Mother had told me the names and descriptions of my best friends, my school friends and what my high school was like. The blankness of any memories of my previous life was ever present within my thoughts. I was fearful of how I would handle anything I might confront. Mother had told me that my friends were looking forward to seeing me again and Susan told her she would help me at school. I wanted to fit into the group of friends Mother had told me I was part of, but I was worried about recognizing so many faces of people I couldn't remember. She told me I might be surprised at how welcoming they would be. She said Susan was especially excited for my return.

On the first day of my return Mother drove me to school. As she parked in front of the entrance, I felt very nervous and fought the desire to escape and go back home where it was safe. I walked into the entrance and to the lockers where Mother had said I'd meet Susan. There was a large group of kids standing around and talking before the starting bell rang.

I heard a voice say, "We heard you were coming back today and we've all been waiting for you." Then someone said, "Welcome back Deedy." "You look great," came from another voice.

"I'm so glad you're here," Susan said as she took my arm and led me down the main hall.

"Hi, Susan. It's good to be back." I lied.

"You look great; your suntan is so dark. You look like you've been to Hawaii or someplace."

"Thanks."

She guided me through the crowds up the stairs to the front hall where I saw several faces that were familiar to me. I could not attach a name to any of the faces, but I was sure I knew them. I said "hello" and greeted each face with a smile.

When the bell rang Susan said, "Deedy, let me see your schedule and I'll walk you to your first class." After reading the names on the small piece of paper I handed her, she smiled saying, "We have the first class together. That's great."

With a sense of relief, I followed her into a classroom already full of faces, some familiar, but most I didn't recognize. Sitting down next to

Susan, we listened for what seemed like hours to a teacher Susan said was named Mr. Blake. Finally a bell rang.

As the day progressed, bell after bell rang and somehow I pushed from class to class, often asking anyone for directions, until finally the three o'clock bell signaled the time to go home had arrived. I met Susan by the school entrance as we had agreed to do earlier. She took hold of my hand saying, "I'll walk you to your mom's car out front. Then I'll be getting a ride home with my boyfriend."

I asked Susan, "Who's your boyfriend?" She answered, "Dick, the same boyfriend I've had for two years. You'll remember him when you see him."

My first day into my new world was finally over and Mother was driving me home.

"How was your first day back at school?" Mother asked as soon as I closed the car door.

"Well, I made it through, but it was like I was in the middle of a sea of people who knew me even though I didn't recognize any of them."

When we reached home I asked if my brother would be home.

"No, he's still at USC. He may be home for the weekend but won't have a real break for a couple of weeks."

That night as I lay safely tucked between the silky pink sheets securely within the walls of my pink flowery room, I quietly cried. The tears poured out from my eyes, wetting my hair and pillow. Four years of troubles spilled out on my bed. Four years of fear, shame, guilt, and confusion. After what seemed like a long time of crying, the tears within my eyes dried up, while, my body still wept. I again asked God to help me. I needed His help if I was going to make my life work.

The moon climbed high into the sky signaling midnight when finally my body emptied itself of the tension that had built up during the day. Soon there was a sense of nothingness as I passed into a deathlike sleep.

❧ ❧ ❧ ❧ ❧

I was floating on a cloud dressed in a filmy white gown with my hair flowing beneath a garland of white petals. There was a beautiful strong handsome man coming toward me with welcoming arms. He was too far away to tell what the features on his face looked like, but he gave the impression of being handsome and I thought he might be my prince charming. Every muscle in his body pulsed as he ran swiftly toward my cloud which was slowly drifting his direction. Soon the features on his face began to become defined until I could clearly see him. A muffled scream came from somewhere as my body began to convulse. He was back coming after me again. Those piercing black eyes were drilling into me. That greasy hair and mustache. I knew I would die this time. My eyes opened and he was no longer in front of me. I didn't die. I am alive and he's gone.

✻ ✻ ✻ ✻ ✻

Slowly, I pulled my body from beneath the twisted sheets and started for the closet where my stash of pills was waiting. I needed something to help me. As I reached into the toe of the shoe, fear of what I was doing began to fill me. I had done this before. I took one of the small yellow pills and held it tightly as I leaned against the wall next to the opened door of the closet. I really needed something. The nightmares had to go away. He had to leave my mind and never return. As I sat on the floor in the dark holding the pill, tears again came flowing from my eyes. I sat for a very long time feeling so very much alone. Will his face follow me the rest of my life? No, I had to push it away. I had to become stronger than his image.

After hours, my body mechanically rose from the floor and carried me into my parent's room. I entered the darkened room and could see my father in his bed nearest the door. The moon was very bright and shadows were cast as it shined through the window. I walked around his bed to where Mother was sleeping in her bed. I stood staring at her for several seconds, then quietly climbed under her covers and nestled close to her warm body.

"Deedy are you alright?" "Did you have a nightmare darling?"

"Yes."

Her warmth made me feel good. The security of her arms protected me.

"Mother, will you help me?"

"Yes, Deedy. I will help you." Her words gave me strength. Gradually my body began to relax as I lay next to her feeling the warmth emanate from her body. The rhythm of her breathing was soothing and soon I drifted off to a warm pleasant sleep while still tightly grasping the little yellow pill. Feeling a cool draft flow around my warm body woke me as Mother quietly slipped out from under the blankets. Not wanting to disturb the peaceful feelings within me, I kept holding my eyelids shut against the morning light. I didn't want the day to begin.

Suddenly I felt the weight of someone sitting next to me on the edge of the bed. I looked up to see my father.

"Deedy, you've had a rough time. For someone so young, life has been cruel. I know something of what you're going through. I know it's difficult to accept the world and trying to find out where you belong!"

I lay very still, trying to grasp what he was saying. "Deedy, I've been watching for some time now and many things have happened of which I don't approve. I never thought you should be in the hospital for so many months. I think you should not have had those shock treatments or the abundance of medicine. You can't hide from the world in a haze of drugs. This world of ours has some very ugly parts. There is too much pain. God made the world we live in and He also made a great amount of beauty for us to enjoy. This is the world God created for us and is the only world we have."

Daddy took a deep breath and looked into my eyes, then continued. "Through the years, I've also had trouble accepting many things that have confronted me, and some time ago I ran across a prayer I often say that has helped me during my low time. This prayer has given me strength and maybe it can do the same for you."

Daddy looked so serious as he recited the prayer, "God, grant me the serenity to accept the things I cannot change, the courage to change the things I can and the wisdom to know the difference."

I looked up to see my father. He sat quietly for some minutes while his words sunk into my mind. What magic words they were. He continued on in a soft, comforting voice, "Now it's time you accept our world the way it is and learn to live in it. Throw away your medicine. Don't go through life in a fog. Use your intelligence and learn to hold your emotions in check while learning to accept what you can't change. Look for the good parts of the world and learn to live next to the bad parts. You don't have to accept the bad parts, but you must not let them take control of you. Now move on with your life and pray to God asking Him to grant you serenity, wisdom, and courage."

I focused on everything Daddy had said to me and thought how wise he sounded. I would try to follow his advice and maybe my life would make sense.

I left the warmth of Mother's bed and got dressed for my second day of school.

As the days moved forward and with Mother's help I worked hard studying the lessons I would have to pass to graduate. When April arrived it began to look like I actually would graduate with my class. I did have a couple of shock treatments, but I was allowed to go home after I woke up and didn't have to stay overnight. Then Mother would drill me with the school lessons that had become fuzzy in my memory. Somehow with her tutoring me, I started to pass tests and moved into the next sections I was supposed to learn.

The month of May had almost arrived and I prepared for my Senior Prom and the graduation ceremony. I had no memory of ever having attended a Prom. I was told I attended one with some boy named Freddy, who Mother had forbidden me to see since I've come home. I went with my friends to the Prom and spent the night going through the motions of looking like I enjoyed myself. A couple of the boys asked me to dance and there too I made it appear I was having a good time.

With the help of well-meaning teachers, my parents and my friends, I was ready to graduate from high school on time with my class. The ceremony seemed false to me because I did not believe I deserved the diploma I was handed.

The most challenging part of this period of time was that I still had very little memory of the lessons I was supposed to have learned while in school. If it hadn't been for the help Mother gave me with my lessons, I knew I would not be graduating. To this day, I believe the teachers had found ways around my lack of ability to remember what they taught me. I started praying for God's help so I would graduate. My prayers were answered by my mother who became the angel who rescued me. She had been involved with the local school system for years and was a highly respected and popular elected member of the Santa Monica Board Of Education. Because of the position she held, she was asked to hand out the certificates at my graduation. I felt I was handed a diploma I had not earned because of whose daughter I was. I gratefully accepted it so that I could move on with my life.

Dr. Branscom still had me as a patient since mother believed what she told her about the dangers of stopping all treatments. I still had shock treatments every now and then. By now I had accepted that I would move on in life without any childhood memories, other than the ones I built from looking at old photographs and listening to the stories my brother told me. I would have to continue forward by relearning most of what I had already been taught. I applied to college knowing that was the best way to refill my mind with the knowledge that the shock treatments had wiped away. By some miracle, after taking and somehow passing the entrance exam I was accepted into college and developed a social life, making new friends, dating, and attending parties.

I went to Junior College for a year and took various classes to refill my mind with knowledge of American and world history, art history, English literature and some philosophy. I thrived in the learning environment I now faced. I was anxious to continue learning and fill my mind with events that were far removed from my past.

By the time I was nineteen I found a loving relationship with my best friend's brother Jim. Kristin and I had become best friends again and she introduced me to Jim who was several years older than either Kristin or me. I was enamored with him and what I perceived as his worldliness. He was kind and gentle and made me feel very loved. Kristin was happy that her brother and her best girlfriend became a twosome. She had continued dating her high school sweetheart, Chuck, up until a year ago. She told me about my boyfriend Freddy and how the four of us double dated before I got sick. I had no memory of Freddy and had not even seen him since I had left the hospital. Kristin had met another man, also named Chuck who she was engaged to marry. I was to be her Maid of Honor and helped with her wedding plans. We talked a lot about marriage and family as she prepared for her new future.

As my relationship with Jim progressed he told me he did not support the belief my mother had that I would need Dr. Branscom's care forever. He kept telling me I was a strong, intelligent girl and should not continue to see her. He did not like the way I acted after the occasional shock treatments Mother still insisted I have. He said I became a zombie. He also wanted me to stop all the drugs Dr. Branscom insisted I needed. This was a tantalizing thought that I wanted to believe could happen. Jim gave me a way out from my current life with his support. Mother and I often argued over my need for shock treatments and whether I needed to continue to see Dr. Branscom. I wanted to believe Jim and still held on to what my father had told me about accepting the world and learning to live in it as it is. With Jim's support, I developed a small amount of confidence in myself and the seeds of a healthy self-esteem began to grow.

I did not want my life to go down the same path I'd followed for several years, which seemed to point nowhere. But I was not quite ready to insist that the drugs and treatments stop.

Jim and I decided we wanted to get married. My parents were strongly against this idea. They told me I was too young to marry and needed more time to grow up and become a confident adult. But I saw it as a way out of the mess my life had become. Many discussions took place with my parents in our living room. We were still in the 1950's and couples did not live with each other until they were married. It was considered 'bad.' I had associated myself with the word 'bad' for so long that marriage was the only way our relationship could grow.

When my parents saw that Jim and I were determined to get married, with or without their approval, they gave in and did everything they could to support our decision. After receiving Mother's and Daddy's hesitant support, Jim and I started to make plans for a life together. We sent out a couple hundred invitations and settled in with great expectations.

My parents made most of the decisions regarding the wedding ceremony and planned a large wedding in the Presbyterian Church. Jim and I were counseled about marriage prior to the ceremony by the Pastor, but as the date came nearer both of us began to question if marriage was the best path for us to take. We went out to dinner to discuss if canceling or postponing the plans should be done. We concluded that it was too late since the invitations had been mailed out and several gifts had already been received. We decided it would be too embarrassing for us to change our minds after working so hard at convincing my parents that this was what we were going to do, even without their blessings.

When the day arrived the weather was beautiful. It was a perfect day with blue sky and the sun shining. We had a large, very formal wedding in a church filled with many beautiful white roses and ribbons. The reception was held around the swimming pool in my parents' backyard with flowers and lighted candles floating in the pool. The reception was catered with all kinds of wonderful food. I felt beautiful dressed in a lacy white wedding dress with a delicate train and veil and had several of my best friends as attendants along with Kristin as my Maid of Honor. Feeling like a princess, I enjoyed the ceremony as I walked down the aisle. The reception was not as enjoyable. Many of the guests were my parents' friends whom I didn't even know. It felt like it was more of a celebration for my parents than for Jim and me. Mother stood next to me in the receiving line introducing many of the guests to me since the majority of them were their friends. After passing through the reception line, most of my close friends took Champagne bottles they sneaked from the back of my house and celebrated amongst themselves. I wanted to leave the reception line and join them, but knowing that would be inappropriate, I did not.

That was how Jim and I started our life together. We received blessings from everyone, but I was unsure if the life we were heading into was the right one for me.

We rented an apartment on San Vicente Boulevard in Santa Monica across the street from where Kristin and her new husband Chuck were renting. Jim raced cars and motorcycles and earned an income working in an auto body shop his father owned. I worked at a dental office making molds of patients teeth. Our relationship during the first several months after the wedding went along fine. We were busy having fun.

After almost five months of marriage, Jim put pressure on me to stop taking what he called 'drugs.' With the encouragement of Jim and the support of my father, I made the decision to flush all my drugs down the toilet. It was a very difficult thing for me to do, but Jim had convinced me I did not need them and deep down inside I knew he was right. With his help, I pushed through the withdrawal. Mother had reservations if this was the best action for me, but gave me her blessings. Looking back I now believe I was more psychologically addicted than physically addicted.

Jim then insisted I stop the shock treatments. Daddy and several of my close friends also thought I should stop them. Stopping the shock treatments was very frightening to me because I feared if Dr. Branscom was correct in her assessment of my condition, I might not be able to cope with all of the demons of my past. I had continued occasional shock treatments while I was attending college, but the results of these experiences had not changed. Not only did I lose my memory, I had to hide it from everyone by becoming very quiet and not participating in conversations. I was willing to think seriously about stopping them and decided to take a week to determine if it was the right move for me.

For days I thought about the effects of the treatments. The electric current that was shot through my brain was so strong that I was left with a horseshoe shaped burn mark on each side of my temples. My curious friends questioned me on what the marks were and how I got them.

I decided to research the history of shock treatments and learned that during a treatment the electricity that was run into my brain with paddle-shaped electrodes was 450 volts, enough to light an 84 watt light bulb for 6 seconds. The shock causes convulsions strong enough to break the bones of patients. To prevent injury all parts of the body were held tight against the bed with rubber straps. A rubber mouth guard is inserted into the mouth to prevent the patient from swallowing their tongue. No wonder they terrified me, especially the times when I was not put to sleep prior to the treatment. My decision was made and with Jim's support and encouragement, a week after our discussion, I took the big step to stop the shock treatments and vowed not to see Dr. Branscom again.

Shortly after separating myself from the shock treatments, drugs, and Dr. Branscom, I went to my parents and asked if they would pay the cost of having me evaluated at UCLA Medical Center. I had to know more about what had happened to me and I needed to know if Dr. Branscom's diagnosis that I would always need psychiatric care was correct. So, with my parents' blessings, I went to one of the top psychiatrists at UCLA and told him of my abduction and rape and of the treatments I had received over the past six years. After giving him the whole story, I asked if he would be willing to evaluate me. He agreed to do a psychiatric assessment and I was set up to go through four days of testing. The analysis consisted of my impression of different pictures and patterns along with a battery of other tests. The following week I had an appointment to see the psychiatrist to find out the results. When I sat down in his office, he asked me what it was I wanted to know. I told him I wanted to know what had happened to me after I was abducted by that man and whether I had actually been crazy. Most importantly, I wanted to know if I should still be seeing a psychiatrist to protect me from going crazy again. I also wanted his opinion on whether my memory would ever return.

The doctor sat quietly for a moment reading the reports he had on the desk in front of him. He looked up at me and proceeded to tell me I had experienced significant trauma in the past which had caused me to partly disassociate from myself. As for my current condition, he said the test indicated I am very grounded and stable. As far as my future, there were no guarantees for anyone. With enough traumatic exposure, anyone could eventually become mentally ill. He went on to tell me that with the unknowns about the effects of electric shock treatments, he was uncertain if my memory would return or not.

Finally, I had the knowledge to back up my decision and consider myself finished with psychiatric treatments and drugs. When I reported the results to my parents, they were not surprised. They both told me that they felt my troubles were behind me and they were so proud of me after everything I had been through. I felt free and in control. I was going to remake myself into someone I would be proud to be.

Approximately six months into our marriage, I started throwing up from early morning until late at night. I was unable to function throughout the day and had to quit my job at the dentist office because my vomiting was uncontrollable. I scheduled an appointment with my doctor and learned I was pregnant. The morning sickness didn't end after the normal three months and I continued to have nausea during the entire nine months and it was miserable.

Concerned about the health of the baby and me, Mother decided to contact Dr. Branscom about my pregnancy. Even though I wasn't a patient of Dr. Branscom's, Mother felt she needed to know the effects this pregnancy could have on me or my unborn child. Dr. Branscom told mother I should not go through with the pregnancy, but should have an abortion. Abortion was illegal at this time, but Dr. Branscom told mother that under the circumstances of my past health problems she would be able to prescribe an abortion for me and could get approval from the courts. When mother told me about this, I was horrified. We talked about it for a long time and Mother confided in me that she was against abortions. She knew I was against them too. We both believe God has created us. Did we have the right to take a life? We both felt it was immoral to take the life of a fetus. The decision was made and I rejected Dr. Branscom's advice.

I delivered my first born son just seven days after turning twenty years old. This forced me to grow up before I was ready. I was still immature in many ways, had not finished college, nor did I have a career. I didn't understand how expensive it was to support a family. I was forced to learn everything quickly. At the age of twenty, I had not settled on a philosophy of how to live and still held some confusion regarding my relationship with God. I started to pray to Him but was not sure if He listened to me. I was still insecure about myself and where I would fit into this grown up world I was in.

Prior to becoming pregnant, I became a follower of Ayn Rand's philosophy of Objectivism. Those who follow Objectivism believe in rational individualism, whereby a person lives by his own effort using reason, purpose, and self-esteem. I believed that I alone was the only one who could make or break any success I might have in life. No outside source would have any influence on the path I might follow, not even God, since I was not sure of His existence in my life. I read every book Ayn Rand wrote and was deeply influenced by the behavior of the characters in Atlas Shrugged and Fountainhead. Objectivism was ruling my life, but I was bothered that God was not included in the philosophy of Objectivism. To me, I thought He should be the one to give the people in the novels the strength to become what they sought.

Even though I still had doubts of how I felt about God or if He cared about me, I decided to have my newly born son baptized. I celebrated Christmas and Easter with my family and there were even Sundays when Jim and I went to church and we talked about God. Jim was sure there was a God. At the same time, I felt I was living a hypocritical life acting as though I believed in God in order to follow popular conventional behavior. However, I still did not feel God in a personal way.

Two years after the birth and baptism of our baby boy, Jim and I were not getting along and I began to understand why my parents had been so against our marriage. Mother and Daddy were right, we were too young. I was grateful for the help Jim had provided and his encouragement to stop shock treatments and pills. I was determined to make our marriage work.

On my twenty-second birthday, the three of us took a trip to the Colorado River that flows between California and Arizona to water ski and camp out under the stars. We were enjoying the summer sun and playing in the water with our little boy when Jim and a few of the other husbands decided to take his boat down the river to a bar. I stayed at our camp with the other wives and my son waiting for the men to return. We prepared dinner for them and waited for their return. As the sun was starting to set Jim and his friends returned and it was apparent they had been drinking heavily. As Jim sat down at the table I placed a plate with a hot dog covered with catchup, mustard, and onions in front of him, then busied myself around the camp site. The next thing I knew, Jim's drunken face plopped down into the middle of his plate, buried in catchup, mustard and onions. As I looked at him, I quietly said to myself, "happy birthday Deedy. Can I live with this man the rest of my life? What will he be teaching our son?"

Without saying anything to Jim, I decided my marriage must be dissolved not only for me but also for our sweet innocent baby boy. He deserved better than what this man could give him. Jim drank often and did not always come home. The longer we were together the more I realized it was time for me to take responsibility for my life and my son's life. The love I felt for my son was a kind of love I hadn't known existed. Everything revolved around him and I wanted to surround him with all the love and time I could provide.

I needed to start earning a living so I enrolled in a business college and learned secretarial skills. When my divorce was final, I did not want any alimony because I was determined to become a success without anyone's help. So I set out on my own with my two-year-old son. I was struggling to become an independent self-supporting single mother and I still lacked self-esteem.

I had a relentless desire to be loved. I craved love and when an opportunity arrived I slept with any attractive man who showed interest in me. Feeling some shame at my questionable behavior I was careful to shield my son and never expose him to what I was doing. I rented a home with another single mother who I had met in high school. We would share the responsibilities of taking care of our children who were the same age. When my room-mate couldn't watch my son, I would take him to my parents' home. That gave me freedom and out on the town to 'party' I'd go. Inevitably I ended up in the arms of a man. This gave me a false sense that someone cared for me.

I was fighting the feeling of failure, which did not fit with the Objectivism philosophy. On the surface, I appeared confident and independent, but inside I was very insecure and had low self-esteem, along with feeling shame for my actions. During the years after that awful man had taken me away, I had learned to fool the world by appearing confident and self-assured, while hiding my feelings. The mannerisms I had developed served me well at this stage of my life. My parents were fooled, my friends were fooled, and the people I worked with were fooled. I was alone with hidden secret feelings of fear and self-loathing and decided I had to get a grip on my promiscuous behavior. My son deserved a wholesome devoted parent to bring him into adulthood.

During the next few years, I worked as an executive secretary to the CEO of an international corporation. I decided I needed to make a change in my life. I was not content with my lack of a professional career, so I approached my parents and asked them if they could help me return to college in order to earn a degree. They agreed. I went back to college. My parents delighted in helping me by watching my son. I had stopped behaving promiscuously and spent more time with my son during weeknights and on weekends. We attended church together and he thrived in Sunday school learning about Jesus.

When I did date, I made it clear to all involved that if anyone was going to become my friend or date me, they would have to accept my son along with my friendship. My son and I became a twosome going everyplace together. When I dated and went places with friends, my son came along. My son has little memory of the various travels he had with me on private airplanes and beautiful boats. I had become involved with a group of young men and women with high morals and standards who respected my relationship with my son. Throughout this time, my son learned that he was my first priority and very much loved.

Months and years moved on and I succeeded in making myself into a young woman I would be proud to know.

A few years later my mother developed breast cancer. She went through mastectomy surgery which brought her ten years of remission. My heart was broken. I was frightened for her and for myself having to live without her. We had become quite close during the past several years and the thought of losing her was devastating. She and I had long discussions about God and she confided in me that she strongly believed in God. She was looking forward to being with her Father and Mother in heaven. She told me she had prayed during all the years of my troubles. I told her I wasn't totally sure how I felt about God or why He had not rescued me from that awful man. I did feel blessed that I had a wonderful son, but what about all the times God didn't rescue me. Mother told me God worked in ways we didn't understand and perhaps He really did rescue me and was with me during all my troubles. Perhaps He was the reason I lived. I had not realized she was so devoted to God.

When I was young she and Daddy had stopped going to church. Prior to that Mother sang in the church choir and since she had a beautiful voice often sang solo at weddings and other ceremonies. I never knew why they stopped going to church and was left unsure of their relationship with God. We occasionally went to a Presbyterian Church as a family, but not consistently and it was a surprise to me when I learned Mother and Daddy believed strongly in God and Jesus.

After Mother and I started talking about God, we had some serious discussions about what we believed. I found out she believed deeply that she would be in heaven with her parents. She confided in me that my grandmother Bambi had a very strong relationship with God and Jesus.

I began to search through my feelings about God but found it only brought me confusion and more questions as to why He had allowed those awful things happen to me.

# Chapter Twenty Nine

## New Life

What I've written so far I consider the first chapter in my journey of life. The events in this chapter started my road to now, which turned out to be a successful journey.

During the next few years I attended college, worked full time and spent free time with my son. I had little social life, but when I learned one of my friends who had a private airplane was flying a group of men to go skiing in Aspen Colorado I decided I wanted to join them. I'd never skied or spent any time in the snow but wanted to take a break from my studies and full-time job. The timing was perfect for me since they were planning the trip during my winter school break in December. I was in dire need of a vacation and if my parents would be willing to watch my son, I would ask to join them. When I told Mother of the opportunity I had she offered to take care of my son while I went on a week's vacation. I contacted my friends to tell them my answer was yes, I could go. They said great as long as I paid for my room and board.

While in Aspen, I met the true love of my life. His name was Wayne Harmala, and he was 11 years older than I was and had never been married, nor had any children. He was an established architect who had flown to Aspen with a group of bachelors with whom he hung out. Since he lived in Minneapolis and I lived in Santa Monica, California we started a long-distance romance after parting in Colorado. During our one week together in Aspen our feelings for each other had grown solid. We developed a deep love for each other from a distance of approximately 2,000 miles while talking on the phone constantly. I visited Wayne in Minneapolis for one week in February and he visited me during my school spring break. After picking him up at LAX, I introduced him to my parents and my son. Wayne had brought some toys for my son and they became fast friends. My son stayed with my parents while Wayne and I drove my car to Mammoth Lakes to go skiing the next day. After a couple of days of skiing, we were enjoying a spaghetti dinner when he asked me to marry him. Even though we had only been physically together a total of fifteen days I immediately said yes. Wayne was a dream come true for me and I felt like our relationship was supposed to happen. He told me he always knew he would marry but up until he met me had not found the right woman. He did not want to delay starting our life together and wanted to have children right away.

When we told my parents we decided we were going to get married, they were very happy for me and believed he would be a wonderful mate for me and father for my son. Daddy developed a special connection to Wayne since they were both architects and after doing a background check of him wholeheartedly approved of our plans to marry. Since Wayne did not want to leave his Minnesota architectural practice in which he was a partner, we both decided I would relocate to Minneapolis with my son where we would be married.

Wayne had wonderful parents who wrote to my seven-year-old son telling him they could hardly wait to meet him and that they already had two granddaughters and were so happy to be getting a grandson.

In July of 1968, we moved to Minneapolis and I became Mrs. Wayne Harmala. My mother, dad, brother and son flew in and participated in our wedding. Wayne wanted a large wedding and made all the preparations for our church wedding and country club reception before I arrived. I was amazed and impressed with the wonderful job Wayne did in organizing our celebration. Everything was beautiful from the flowers at the church and reception, the dinner and wine served, down to the beautifully carved ice swan on the wedding cake table. It was a fairy tale start of our new family together. My mother and father kept my son with them for the wedding night while Wayne and I spent our first night as husband and wife in a luxury hotel.

My seven-year-old son became our son when Wayne formally adopted him. We had become a complete family, all with the same last name.

Ten months after the wedding, our second son was born. It was a difficult birth, with extreme complications.

During the early 1960's when I delivered my first son, many obstetricians including the group I was seeing acted as though it was unnecessary to burden pregnant women with details they did not need know. I had not been consulted about delivery choices or what to expect and was put under general anesthesia.

When I awoke in the recovery room I asked the doctors who were kneading my stomach, when was I going to have my baby? I was shocked when they advised me that I had already delivered a healthy baby boy. I was saddened to learn I missed the entire experience of the actual birth of my first son and as a result by the time my second son was born, it was like a first-time delivery experience. I had learned nothing from my first time around other than I vomited for nine months and hurt after the delivery.

During my second pregnancy, I was in a very loving relationship with Wayne. When getting prepared for my second delivery, the doctors provided me with the information they felt was necessary in order to prepare me for the delivery procedure and I was very excited and looked forward to the event.

In the first couple of months of my second pregnancy, the obstetrician said he thought he heard two heartbeats. During the 1960's there was no way to see visually what was happening inside the womb since diagnostic imaging (ultrasound) was not commonly used. There was no way to verify twins would be born. As the pregnancy progressed the second heartbeat disappeared and the obstetrician said what he heard had probably been an echo, and we prepared for a single birth. When the delivery day arrived, I was completely alert during the entire labor and delivery of a big healthy baby boy.

During this time period, women who delivered babies in a hospital were expected to remain in the hospital for at least one week, which turned out to be exactly where I needed to be when my next experience hit me.

Two days after the delivery I started having extreme pain and a high fever. The pain in my lower abdomen was horrendous, and my fever was rising. I had many different tests to pinpoint the problem. There was no diagnosis. On the fourth day after delivery, I was nursing my son, when I looked down and saw a huge amount of blood was pouring from between my legs. I called out to my roommate "get help! Quickly! Something is terribly wrong!" I laid my baby down between my legs trying to protect him as I began fading away. A nurse peeked in the door, took one look at me and ran back out. Suddenly a large group of doctors and nurses burst into the room and proceeded to take my baby off the bed as I felt the head of my bed was pushed down with the foot end raised up.

# Chapter Thirty

# God Reached Down and Saved Me

I could hear everyone who was working on me, but could not see them, feel them, nor move my body. I was totally numb with zero strength. I tried to move my little finger, but could not. I knew I was fading into nothing, but could still hear them talking to me. I heard, "You're fine Deedy. You're going to be fine," when suddenly I felt myself falling into a dark spiraling tunnel that felt wonderfully welcoming. The tunnel was like a magnet calling me into it, and I wanted to go. It felt like the most wonderfully peaceful place as I slowly floated down into the tunnel. I was in a peaceful darkness when a large gentle male hand appeared from the bright light at the entrance of the tunnel above my head and reached down toward me. I had a strong sense that the hand wanted me to grab hold of it. I had a choice to make; reach toward the welcoming hand or let my body fall into the tunnel. The draw of the hand was very powerful and was pulling at me while the tunnel was also beckoning to me. I had to choose which way to go. The pull of the hand was more powerful than the tunnel.

I knew I couldn't reach the hand physically with my immovable hand so if I wanted to grasp it I had to do it with my thoughts. I forced my thoughts to push my mind up to reach the hand. Then suddenly I was back on the hospital bed with strong hands kneading my stomach which was painful. "What's happening?"

Next thing I knew I was rolled over to one side of the mattress and my bedding was being changed. After my bed and I were cleaned up, I was shaking with emotion and asked the doctor "what happened? Did I die?" He said "there were a few seconds that were touch and go, but everything is in control now. You are fine and don't have to worry."

"I want my husband. I need to see him. Please call him for me. Tell him I need him."

Wayne came shortly after he was called and came to my bedside. He grasped my hand saying, "I talked to the doctor and you're going to be fine now. What happened was good and now they know why you had so much pain and a fever."

"Wayne, I think it was God's hand reaching for me. He wants me to live."

"Of course He does Deedy. We have a beautiful baby boy who needs his mother. I need you too and God made sure you will be here for us."

The next morning the doctor surgically went into my womb and found a hard blister-like cast that had adhered to the wall of my womb and contained the remains of a dead fetus. Apparently my pregnancy had begun with twins, but one had died and to protect the one still living, my body had built a protective wall separating the dead fetus from the living fetus. The hemorrhaging had occurred because my body was trying to rid itself of the remains still inside the womb.

I was overcome with a tremendous emotional upheaval. I knew in my heart that the hand reaching down the tunnel had been God's. He wanted me to live. I was overwhelmed by this experience, and I asked to see the pastor. Did he think God had brought me back? Why? When I had been so awful toward Him and had even doubted He existed. Why would He want me to live? The pastor said God works in ways we don't understand. But, yes he believed it was God's hand that brought me back. When Wayne came in to see me after I had talked to the pastor, we talked about what had happened. I had always known Wayne had a very strong faith, and believed God was always with him. He did not find my experience surprising because he believed God is with all of us at all times. My roommate was a strong Catholic, and we talked for some time. She also believed God was with me. No one could say why, or what God had planned for me or my son, but everyone who had faith believed that what had happened was a miracle from God.

At the time, which was 1969, I had not heard of near death experiences, but in recent years many stories of people who have gone through similar events have been published. I came to believe God is active in our lives and that He reached down to me because He wanted me and my son alive.

My heart had been deeply touched. I began to look back at my life and wondered if God had been with me at other times. Could it be that I had lived through several horrific events because God did save me? My view of God softened and I started to pray to Him.

After recovering for three weeks in the hospital, I went home with my second baby son. An adorable blond baby with wonderful blue eyes.

A couple of years later I was four months pregnant with our third child when my Mother became terminally ill with cancer which had returned a couple of years earlier. I flew to California to be with her the last few weeks of her life, and we talked a great deal. We shed many tears while discussing the past. She apologized for going along with Dr. Branscom's treatment of me. She told me Dr. Branscomb had been highly recommended and that she had put too much faith in the doctor believing she must know the best treatment I required to heal. It was obvious that I was very mixed up and needed professional help, but the drugs, ice baths, and shock treatments were probably not what I should have gone through. I hugged mother and told her I forgave her and understood she was trying to help and protect me. I told her I loved her so much and that she was the best mother I could possibly have ever had. She was like a gift from God the way she helped me and devoted so much time working with me.

When I apologized for the bad way I had treated her, she said she understood and was at peace. She said she was also at peace with God and not afraid to die. She told me she was looking forward to joining her mother again. Her deep faith and peaceful passing left a positive mark on me. I felt very close to Mother when at the age of 63 she closed her eyes for the last time. I prayed that she knew how wonderful my life was turning out. After the burial ceremony which brought many more tears knowing I would never hug her again, I returned to my growing family in Minneapolis to finish out the remaining months of my third pregnancy.

In 1971 I delivered our third beautiful baby boy. I had always wanted the experience of bringing up a little girl, but when I saw my adorable third son I fell in love. It was not to be part of my journey to become the mother of a girl. I happily settled with three healthy boys, and we had no more babies. Our family was set and full of love.

As time moved on, Wayne designed and built a beautiful home for us which we moved into just before our first son entered junior high school. We were a complete family who lived in a beautiful home built by my beloved husband in a lovely wooded setting. What else could I ask for?

Years passed and after all my boys were in school questions that had remained in my thoughts surrounding my past began to resurface. The mental anguish and confusion after my kidnapping still lingered in my mind. I also had many unanswered questions regarding the near-death experience after the birth of my second son. My thoughts of God were still confused. When trying to describe to Wayne or any of my close friends the kidnapping and the horrible experiences I went through after surviving, I would start to tremble. I would stutter and stammer and started to feel cold as my shaking would not stop. It was almost impossible for me to describe the traumatic events and how they affected me, because when talking about them, it was almost as if I was reliving them.

Wayne suggested I write my life story down and maybe it would act like a catharsis resolving many of my issues. I started by talking into a tape recording machine, but that didn't work. I found myself becoming too emotional. Then I tried hand writing the words, but that was also too emotional, and too slow. Next, I tried typing the story, which was much better. During this effort, I was busy bring up our boys and could not devote much time to my story. Periodically I attempted to work on it but would end up putting the effort aside and try not to think about it. But I continuously had a nagging thought in my mind that I should do something positive with my experiences. I would again bring out the typewriter and start typing. Eventually, when computers became common in homes I bought one and started to make real progress on my story.

Why did I go through such torment? Why did my mind become so unstable after I was kidnaped? At one time Dr. Branscomb told my mother that I may have schizophrenia, but that proved to be false. What had happened to my mind? What caused me to escape into a fantasy world through delusional thinking? Why was I so out of touch with reality? What had happened to my cognitive processes? It was obvious I was very confused regarding what had happened to me and had created a misconstrued reason as to why it even happened. It was not a common practice to counsel victims of rape in the 1950's, and with no immediate counseling my mental confusion and thought processes grew out of control. By the time I developed feelings of guilt, antisocial tendencies and skewed perceptions of reality, I badly needed medical help. Looking back I believe the treatment I received once I was under the care of a Dr. Branscom may have had a negative impact on me and made my condition even worse. The many shock treatments and large amount of drugs I received could very well have harmed me. The broken jaw that occurred when I fell may have been what saved me from further damage and precipitated my final emotional healing. Even though I went through a form of hell, I am thankful that I didn't receive another type of treatment that was used during the 1950's, which was the neurosurgical procedure of lobotomy. I eventually recognized that God was with me during my healing and gave me the strength to fight my way into mental stability and a healthy life.

My story was put on the back burner as my boys were growing up. I was now a happily married woman with three sons and in-laws I learned to love. I saw the strong faith they had and craved to feel as confident about God and life as they did. I already knew Wayne had an unwavering faith. He had told me our lives are in God's hands. He would say, it's all up to God." I asked my mother-in-law what she had done to instill such a deep faith in Wayne. She answered, "Nothing. He was born believing and has never changed."

As a family we attended a Lutheran Church and one day when I met with the pastor I burst out crying telling him of my traumatic youth. He recognized that I still held anger toward God, so he set me up with an appointment with a special Lutheran Church that tends to those who have experienced sexual abuse. The pastors who worked at this church were ordained pastors who were also trained as psychological counselors.

I met with a male and a female pastor who were very warm and made me relax. We sat and talked, and soon words flew out of my mouth exposing my anger at God for allowing so many horrible things to happen to me.

The male pastor stood up and asked me to stand up next to him and tell God through him what I was feeling. I opened my mouth and started crying and soon I was yelling at God asking why didn't He rescue me. Why had He let me go through such terrible experiences? I even hit the pastor's chest as I yelled and screamed at God. My anger flowed from me until I was empty of all emotions. As soon as I recomposed myself fear swept over me about the awful way I had just yelled at God and the terrible things I had said. The pastor told me God understood and that it was good that I had been honest with God. I asked if he thought God would forgive me. The pastor told me I was already forgiven, and now it was time for me to start trusting God and He would complete my healing. God had always been with me and probably the reason I was alive was because God wanted me to live.

❧ ❧ ❧ ❧ ❧

In 2009, I faced one last traumatic event that could have tested my new found faith. My second son, with whom I had my near death experience and had felt God's touch after his delivery, had grown into a loving husband and father of three young children. He was a Med-Peds physician who worked in a top hospital in Minnesota, when at the age of 39 he was diagnosed with cancer and died nine months later. There was nothing sadder in my life than to watch my beloved second son die way before he should. I went through my grieving process and two years later realized how wonderfully blessed my life had been to have had this wonderful son for 40 years. Now I thank God in my prayers that John had been a part of our family on earth for 40 years, and I've asked God to keep him safe in heaven so I can hug him again.

Last Chapter

# Closing

I had touched death and survived three times. Even though I did not realize it at the time, God had held me through the survival of a broken neck and kidnapping. He saved me from death and brought healing to me. When I became so confused and sick that I could not find my path God guided me back. After hemorrhaging from the birth of my second son He even reached His hand down and pulled me out of the tunnel in which my life would have ended.

From that point on I delved into the Bible and learned what God's Words said to me. I soon became a woman with self-confidence, self-esteem, and a positive and grateful attitude. I brought God into my life 24/7 and have felt His love in a very personal way ever since.

Life is a journey, and everyone has negative experiences which can cause trauma and stymie their progress forward. But when we walk and talk with God, He brings us the peace we all crave. It wasn't until I completely accepted God and trusted that the He was with me throughout all the traumas I experienced and was healed by Him.

When I was bringing my sons up, we attended church but did not discuss God as I now wish we had. I wasn't ready. I still carried the scars that were very deep and was not able to share what I learned later about faith. I pray the Holy Spirit will give my two remaining sons and all my wonderful grandchildren the message that God is watching them and walking with them through their journey on earth. That when they confront troubling times, life will smooth out sooner if they communicate with, and ask God for His help. It would be good to know they pray and are thankful to God for their time on earth. Peace will fill them when their faith is strong.

Since life is a journey filled with learning, experiences, and coming to conclusions about how to live, with trust in the Lord comes peace.

*Deedy and Wayne became husband and wife in 1968*

*Deedy and Wayne happily married for 49 years and looking forward to celebrating their 50th Anniversary in 2018.*

# Thank You

A deeply felt thank you goes to Edna Siniff of Elderberry Publishing, for encouraging and guiding me to the completion and publication of my story.

After close to 40 years of writing and reliving my story I was unable to come to the last chapter. One Sunday I was sitting in church feeling over-whelmed and discouraged so I prayed to God asking Him to give me a sign. Should I continue or should I stop writing? Had writing my story served the much-needed purpose as a cleansing catharsis? The next day I received a phone call from a friend telling me about a publisher named Edna Siniff who was interested in my story.

That was the beginning of a wonderful friendship with a guiding angel named Edna, which produced this book.

Thank you Edna. I will always be grateful to you!

CPSIA information can be obtained
at www.ICGtesting.com
Printed in the USA
FFOW04n1701091017
40868FF